Designer Cards & Tags

WITH

K&COMPANY
LLC

Designer Cards & Tags

WITH

K&COMPANY
LLC

BY

Tracey Niehues

A LARK/CHAPELLE BOOK

A Division of Sterling Publishing Co., Inc.
New York

A Lark/Chapelle Book

Chapelle, Ltd., Inc., P.O. Box 9252, Ogden, UT 84409
(801) 621-2777 • (801) 621-2788 Fax
e-mail: chapelle@chapelleltd.com
Web site: www.chapelleltd.com

10 9 8 7 6 5 4 3 2 1

First Edition
Published by Lark Books, A Division of
Sterling Publishing Co., Inc.
387 Park Avenue South, New York, N.Y. 10016

Distributed in Canada by Sterling Publishing,
c/o Canadian Manda Group, 165 Dufferin Street
Toronto, Ontario, Canada M6K 3H6
Distributed in the United Kingdom by GMC Distribution Services,
Castle Place, 166 High Street, Lewes, East Sussex, England BN7 1XU
Distributed in Australia by Capricorn Link (Australia) Pty. Ltd.
P. O. Box 704, Windsor, NSW 2756, Australia

ISBN 13: 978-1-57990-986-4
ISBN-10: 1-57990-986-8

For information about custom editions, special sales, premium and corporate
purchases, please contact Sterling Special Sales Department at 800-805-5489 or
specialsales@sterlingpub.com.

Table of Contents

At our core, K&Company is driven by design. We are passionate about creating beautiful details that stand the test of time. So, when we met Tracey Niehues, we were immediately taken with how her remarkable work aligned with our tried-and-true philosophy. She uses our products in ways that prove to be both charming and daring, and she creates richly dimensional projects, which I love. Tracey has become one of our most trusted designers, crafting and teaching projects for K&Company all over the world.

Tracey's work celebrates the creative process, uniting inner imagination and outward appeal. Her projects beckon viewers to interact with dangling charms, bow-tied ribbons, pocketfuls of secrets, and layers of unexpected details. She turns a simple greeting card into a treasured gift, a tag into a tiny masterpiece. This knack for piecing together something spectacular comes naturally to Tracey. For the rest of us, it serves as a welcome breath of inspiration.

Kay Stanley

Foreword

Introduction

As a scrapbooker and product designer for K&Company, I generally spend my creative time making large-scale projects. So when I set out to create the designs for this book, I was excited at the prospect of making several cards and tags—or as I came to view them, "little pieces of art." Each project invited a new idea, a distinct look and feel, and a different sentiment from the last one. I enjoyed the creative process that went into each one.

The appeal of handmade cards and tags is not only aesthetic. These handcrafted pieces allow us to connect with others in a more significant way than if we had just chosen a card off the rack. Handmade cards mean more to the people you give them to because you have taken the time to create them yourself. When I make a card for someone, I like to personalize it with photographs, the recipient's favorite things, funny sayings that we share, and other touches that hold meaning for both of us. When I'm giving something that may be a little impersonal— like a gift card or store-bought item—a handmade enclosure is a way to put more of myself into the gift.

In fact, I like to think of my cards as gifts in themselves because of the time and attention that goes into creating them. With cards and tags, the beauty and appeal lie in the details, and because the projects are small, you can spend more time on those details. When I create these "little pieces of art," I take time to add dimension and depth with distressed papers, textures, embellishments, and substantial lettering. Because I enjoy creating something that looks loved, I find myself drawn again and again to the timeworn appearance of vintage and retro styles.

Designing and K&Company

When it comes to creating, I'm what they call a "slow scrapbooker" because I put a lot of thought into each project. I'm always thinking about what I can do differently to make it perfect. I have a vision when I create, and to make that vision perfect takes me a little longer. The logical side of my brain isn't content to let the creative side totally take over. Believe it or not, it hasn't been until recently that the creative side became a major part of my life. Although I have always enjoyed making things—my mom and I had always crafted together—I didn't pursue art as a career until much later in life. In college, I went after something completely different: business. I took art classes too, and, even though the school's art director tried to persuade me to go into graphic design or advertising, I chose to earn my degree in accounting.

Yet art did win out, eventually. I was working in a clerical job in the rural Kansas town where my husband, Bob, and I lived when my mom introduced me to something she said would be "right up my alley." It was scrapbooking. After a few scrapbooking parties, I was hooked. Six months later, my husband and I were living in Kansas City where my mom worked at a local scrapbooking store. I attended classes at the store and started teaching

there. One night, Kay Stanley happened to visit the store and my relationship with K&Company began. She told me about her vision to do a vintage look for a new product line and told me that my style would be a perfect fit.

She was absolutely right. Working for K&Company is indeed a great fit. I am delighted to be designing products for the richly textured, vintage-inspired lines that represent the K&Company look. Kay Stanley has a great vision. She is intelligent, down-to-earth, and the sweetest person I have ever met. Although K&Company has developed into a large, successful business, the atmosphere is still relaxed, the people are still warm and friendly, and most importantly, the company is still driven by art.

Since 2003, I have been creating K&Company products, including *Seams to Me*, a line of adhesive decorative borders with zigzag stitching; *Suddenly Stitched*, a line of ribbons with zigzag stitching; and several blank accordion books and tag books. In addition to designing products, I attend trade shows and expos and teach scrapbooking classes for K&Company. These activities help me continue to find new designs and techniques to use on handmade cards and tags.

The Creative Process

I approach design the way I would a puzzle, looking for just the right things to fit the look and feel I'm aiming for. Whether your inspiration comes from a product, a quote, a song lyric, or just an idea, I encourage you to start with your vision for the project then determine what products will achieve that vision. For a 1950s look, think clean lines, geometrics, punchy colors, and perhaps a glossy finish. A vintage look calls for muted colors, aged papers, old-fashioned images, and rich textures.

Introduction

Try using non-traditional products when you create. I find some items for my projects at the hardware store. At trade shows, I've even been known to rip cardboard off boxes and strings off crates—anything is game. You can also explore and combine products in unusual ways. For example, if I have a K&Company product in front of me, like a metal rod, I might turn it into a hinge. One card I created needed a large buckle, so I combined a frame and a rod to make one.

How to Use This Book

This book is intended to inspire you, give you ideas, and teach you tricks for achieving a beautiful, polished look when creating your own cards and tags. The following chapter contains a description of materials and techniques to guide you. For the beginner, I have included a list of items you'll need and a walk-through of cardmaking basics. For the advanced crafter, there's information on my favorite specialized materials and techniques. Where appropriate, the instructions for each project include the product numbers for the specific item or kit I used. These numbers are presented in parentheses after the generic name and, unless otherwise noted, refer to a K&Company product. This is for those of you who wish to achieve exactly the same look pictured, but feel free to use other materials if you wish. Your cards and tags can still turn out great.

These pages are filled with card and tag ideas for any occasion and for any recipient, from family members to good friends to anyone else on your cardgiving list. You will find cards and tags that celebrate births and birthdays, along with sentiments for those times you want to say "I love you" and those times you need to say "Thanks." I have also included vintage and retro projects for the holidays. Of course, the beauty of handmade cards is that you can customize them for any event. Use these projects as inspiration to create something personal for your friends and family. Not only will you enjoy the process, but you will also be able to connect with those you care about through the gift of your time, thoughtfulness, and the act of sharing something beautiful.

Materials and Techniques

The projects in this book range from ones that use materials that are familiar to most paper crafters to ones that are somewhat more complex. To help you get started, this chapter explains the basic items needed to create most of the projects, plus a list of what you'll need when you're ready to expand your creative horizons. Then it describes my favorite techniques for adding rich detail to handmade cards and tags.

Basic Materials

Readily available at craft stores, these items are the foundation of the cardmaker's supply box.

Awl

A long metal spike with a handle, this tool is useful for creating holes for brads and to hand-sewn stitches. In a pinch, an embroidery needle can be used, but many crafters find they work faster and more comfortably with an awl.

Cardstock

This heavyweight paper provides stability and is the foundation for cardmaking, whether used alone or as a backing for lighter weight papers. Most of my cards and tags begin with ivory or black cardstock.

Chipboard

Chipboard is a paper product that is not as thick and bulky as cardboard, but is heavier than cardstock. When I create a card with heavy embellishments, I use chipboard for added stability. Many everyday items (such as cereal boxes) are made of chipboard.

Craft Glue

Use this liquid glue on things that require more hold than a paper-to-paper adhesive will give, such as trims, fabric, ribbons, and chipboard. Look for a brand of that is versatile and strong enough to hold several types of materials, including metal.

Craft Knife

Use this tool to cut paper and cardstock whenever using scissors would be difficult, like when cutting a window in a card cover or when cutting out stickers that have been applied to cardstock as you can maneuver more easily around curved edges and interior spaces.

  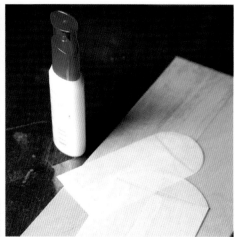

Craft Scissors

A high-quality, sharp pair of craft scissors is indispensable in cardmaking. Aim for scissors with a small tip for more precise cutting.

Cutting Mat

This is a special mat that won't harm your craft knife blade while shielding a work surface from cuts, scratches, paint, glue, or ink. Many come marked with grids to help you cut straighter lines.

Dye Inkpads

Dye ink is fade-resistant and water-resistant. Designed primarily for use with rubber stamps, inkpads can also be used with sponges, cosmetic pads, and other tools to add color to projects.

Gel Superglue

The gel formula of this adhesive means it won't drip. The tiny applicator tip and extra-strong hold make it ideal for small objects that require just a dot of glue, as well as for heavier embellishments, such as metal items.

Hole Punch

This tool is a must when you want to hang items from a card or tag. Hole punches come in different diameters. The common office hole punch is $1/4"$, perfect for many projects, but a $1/8"$ punch is better when smaller holes are required. Thread ribbon, string, jump rings, or wire through punched holes then hang tags, charms, or other embellishments.

Old Books

Pages from old books can be cut apart and used for text or as background paper in projects. Not only can it be fun to search for words to create the popular "ransom note" look, the old book pages may be nicely aged and contain unusual and appealing fonts. Just make sure you're not cutting apart a rare first edition!

Paper Trimmer

This measuring/cutting tool is an absolute must if you are serious about making more than a few cards at a time. Though you certainly can make cards without it, I believe that every paper crafter needs one. It saves time by allowing you to measure and cut at the same time, and often with more accurate results than you'd get cutting by hand.

Patterned Papers

Patterned papers create the mood of a project the way wallpaper can set the mood of a room. Sold in kits, packages, and as individual sheets, patterned papers are fun to shop for and even more fun to use.

Pigment Ink Markers and Pens

Pigment ink writing tools are waterproof, fade-proof, and non-bleeding. I use them for titles, subtitles, handwritten sentiments, and detailing. You can also use them to create the look of dimension by drawing shadows around a letter or motif.

Ruler

Crucial for measuring and as a straight edge, a ruler can also be used with a stylus to score paper. Holding it firmly in place, run the stylus along side its edge (see "Stylus," below, for more instruction).

Stamps

Stamps are an easy way to add lettering, images, or patterns to paper and are especially useful when you wish to create a lot of cards quickly. Alphabet stamps come in handy for card titles.

Stylus

This pen-like tool features a blunt point that makes it ideal for scoring cards before folding. Simply lay a ruler over the card where you want the fold, and run the stylus along the straight edge of the ruler. The indent made by the stylus will become the outside spine of the card.

Tape Runner Adhesive

Tape runners feature a thin strip of double-sided tape in a dispenser that makes it ideal for quick application. The low moisture content of tape runner adhesive means it won't buckle paper, as craft glue often can, making it my preferred means of adhering paper to paper.

maintain a polished look when affixing acetate to a project, use stitching, brads, eyelets, staples, or tape placed behind solid borders, titles, or embellishments. Because acetate is a non-porous material, be sure to use permanent ink if trying to print or stamp on it.

Acrylic Paint

With so many colors of paint available, it is easy to change any embellishment to fit a project. Paint can add texture and depth as well as color, and can be used much like ink for distressing materials and stamping images.

Brown Shoe Polish

This is a simple but effective material for giving new paper products an aged look. Apply it with a soft cloth, concentrating on the edges.

Clear Dimensional Adhesive

This material dries to a clear, glassy, raised finish. It can be used as an adhesive or just to give a glassy layer of dimension to a project.

Corner Rounder

This is a paper punch that trims right angles into a rounded shape. Rounded edges give a tag or card a less rigid look and slide into pockets, sleeves, and envelopes easier than square edges do.

Foam Tape

With a layer of adhesive on both sides of a strip of foam, this tape is a fast and easy way to add three-dimensional effects to cards and tags. Readily available in grocery stores as well as craft stores, foam tape comes in various widths and can be cut to size.

Special Materials

To create some of the projects in this book, I drew from a number of items that are not absolutely necessary for creating great cards, but which I often turn to when I want to add that singular detail to a card or tag that makes it unique.

Acetate

Acetate is a transparent sheet that can be placed over photos and patterned paper to add depth and interest. To

Gel Medium

Gel medium can be used as an adhesive, a transfer medium, and a sealer. I tend to use a matte finish, but it is also available in a gloss finish for when you want some shine.

Glassine Envelopes

Glassine envelopes are made from translucent paper are useful for holding gift cards and money enclosures. They can be crumpled for texture, stamped, painted, or inked.

Jump Rings

Jump rings are metal rings typically used to connect jewelry pieces. However, they also come in handy for attaching dangling elements to cards through a punched hole.

Manicurist's Cosmetic Pads

Available on the Internet and at some beauty supply stores, these handy items have lint-free felt on one side and a plastic tab on the other. Designed to protect a manicurist's fingers while removing a client's nail polish, these pads are perfect for smoothly applying ink to give a project an aged look. If you have difficulty finding them, you can use a cotton ball or a clean rag, though the results don't tend to be as smooth.

Model Paint

Model paint adheres well to metal, making it my first choice for tasks such as changing the color of brads. It also comes in several metallic shades, which is great when you want the look of metal without the weight.

Sandpaper

Super fine grit sandpaper is a great way to distress paper and stickers. Just rub the sandpaper lightly across the material until the desired effect is achieved. Pair this technique with a little brown shoe polish for an instant vintage look.

Sewing Machine

This is a great tool for creating pockets, attaching acetate, and adding texture and detail. For an inexpensive option, look for a machine that sews basic stitches only.

Scoring Board

This board has a centering ruler, enabling you to find your mark easily to produce a very professional-looking fold quickly. The investment is particularly worth it if you want to make cards often or in large quantities.

Stapler and Staples

Staples can be decorative as well as functional, providing a quick and interesting way to attach fabric, ribbon, acetate, and paper to cards.

Watercolor Pencils

Used dry, watercolor pencils act like ordinary colored pencils, but if you brush water over the marks, the lines dissolve into a watercolor paint effect. You can also dip the tip of the pencil in water and draw with it that way. I find watercolor pencils are particularly useful for adding shadows around the edges of stickers.

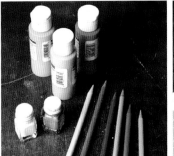

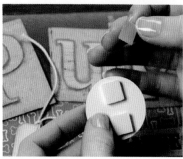

Techniques

Truly special cards call for an attention to detail. Basic techniques done well plus a few slightly more advanced methods will help you present your creations with polish and flair.

Aging Paper

A touch of brown ink, paint, or shoe polish adds age, depth, and warmth to paper and other materials. To apply ink or diluted paint, dab a cotton ball or manicure pad into the color, then rub it over the paper. I tend to use shoe polish on smaller areas, such as letters, applying it with a clean rag.

Applying Rub-on Transfers

The key to neat, professional-looking transfers is taking the time to apply them carefully and thoroughly. To do this, cut around the image to be transferred. Remove the backing sheet and position the transfer on the desired surface. Rub over the image with the end of a wooden craft stick, covering the entire area. Slowly peel the sheet back while checking the image for transfer. If any part of the image begins to peel up with the sheet, lay the sheet back down and rub over that area until the entire image is transferred.

Attaching Jump Rings

Opening jump rings the correct way will help prevent them from breaking. To open a jump ring, use two pairs of needle-nosed pliers to hold the ring on either side of the split. Bring one end toward you while pulling the other end away from you. Reverse this process to close the jump ring.

Building Dimension

There are different ways to help elements stand out in a project. You can create actual three-dimensional layers or use shading to create the look of dimension. One of my favorite methods for creating dimension is to adhere a sticker to cardstock, cut it out using a craft knife, and attach the mounted sticker to the project using foam tape.

Creating Rough Edges

Tearing or distressing the edges of paper gives them an interesting weathered look. I like to use sandpaper to rough up the edges of paper. I also use it to "cut" paper. To do this, adhere a piece of paper to a metal or chipboard backing, then rub the sandpaper over the edges until you have worn through the paper. The paper will be "cut" around the shape of the backing. You can also create straight torn edges placing a ruler on top of the paper and tearing the paper along the ruler's edge.

Cutting Out Windows

A "window" cut from the cover of the card is a neat detail. To do this, first trace a template onto the inside cover with a pencil. Using a craft knife and a steady hand, cut along the outside of the pencil line. When you remove the interior paper, the pencil line is removed as well. If you will be placing a frame around the window, use the interior edges of the frame as a template. For circular windows, you can buy templates or simply use everyday objects like cups.

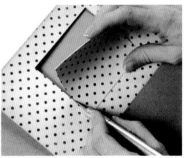

Making Hinged Cards

While a traditional card consists of one piece of paper that is folded over, a hinged card contains two pieces connected together. To make a hinged card, stack two pieces of paper or cardstock and punch two or three holes along the edge. Connect the pieces of paper through the holes using jump rings, ribbons, metal hinges, etc.

Peeling Paper

This simple technique uses masking tape to strip away layers of paper, giving it a tattered, worn look. To use, place a piece of masking tape across the paper and rub the back of the tape with a blunt tool. As you slowly pull the tape off, it peels away the top layer of paper. Repeat with a new strip of tape, if desired.

Materials and Techniques

Family Time

A handmade gift is, first and foremost, a gift of love. Who better to give your love to than your family? When you create a personalized card or a gift tag especially for family members, they know that you've paid attention to the little things that make them who they are. Whether for Mother's Day, Father's Day, or any time you want to lift the spirits of a loved one, a handmade card can strengthen family ties even more.

Grandpa Tag

Pay tribute to a special person in your life by featuring him on a tag. The vintage look of this design is a perfect match for a black-and-white photo that will remind Grandpa of his younger years.

Materials

— ⅛" hole punch
— Black and white photograph
— Chipboard
— Craft glue
— Craft scissors
— Domed map sticker (557697)
— Eyelet setter and black eyelet
— "Grandpa" embossed sticker (551763)
— Hanging rod (558410)
— Large jump ring
— Lock and key charms (558373)
— Metal buttons with holes
— Oval brass frame (563490)
— Ribbon
— String
— Tape runner adhesive
— Vintage-style label (670167)

Directions

1. Apply the vintage-style label onto chipboard. Cut the chipboard to be slightly larger than the label.

2. Apply the domed map sticker to the top of the tag and punch a hole through its center. Set the eyelet in the hole and tie a ribbon through it.

3. Adhere the oval brass frame to the photograph and trim the photograph to fit. Apply craft glue to the back of the frame and adhere it to the tag.

4. Attach the keys to the hanging rod with a jump ring. Use craft glue to adhere the hanging rod to the tag.

5. Thread a length of string through the holes in a metal button and adhere it to the tag. Tie the opposite end of the string through the holes in a second button and adhere it to the tag. Apply the "Grandpa" embossed sticker to the tag.

Family Time

Mother Card

I love to use large text in my projects, so I went a step further with this one and made the entire card one letter. You can adapt this design to any letter in the alphabet by using the same technique.

Materials

— Aqua tulle
— Beads
— Craft glue
— Craft scissors
— Die-cut letter stickers (553347)
— Doll pin (558427)
— Ivory cardstock (630918)
— Large jump ring
— Metal word charm (250000)
— M pattern (page 141)
— Needle and thread
— Pink satin fabric
— Polka-dotted paper (661080)
— Ribbon
— Ruler
— Tape runner adhesive

Directions

1. Score and fold the ivory cardstock in half to make a card, then trace the M pattern onto the card, making certain that the top of the letter is at the fold. Add stability to the card by cutting a second M from chipboard and adhering it to the back of the card with tape runner adhesive.

2. Trace the M pattern onto polka-dotted paper. Cut out the paper and adhere to the card cover using tape runner adhesive.

3. Apply the die-cut letter stickers M, T, H, E, and R on the card, leaving space for the O.

4. Cut out a circle from pink satin fabric. Knot one end of the thread and sew a running stitch around the edge of the circle. Hem the edge under $1/8$" before each stitch is made. Pull the thread to gather the fabric into a ruffled circle. Make several small stitches at the center and knot the end to secure.

5. Cut a square from the aqua tulle. Use craft glue to adhere it to the card, then to adhere the fabric circle to the tulle.

6. Attach a jump ring to the metal word charm and thread it onto the doll pin. Stick the pin through the fabric circle. Place beads onto the pin, then replace the pin cap. Tie a ribbon to the pin.

Family Time

Mother's Day Card

Look beyond the obvious to find unique solutions for your projects. This card uses a hanging rod attached to a chipboard die-cut frame to achieve the large impact of a belt buckle without the weight of a metal embellishment.

Materials

— Brown floral paper (661158)
— Craft glue
— Craft scissors
— Die-cut oval frame
— Gel superglue
— Green patterned paper (661134)
— Ivory cardstock (630918)
— Jewels
— "Mother's Day" tag (564466)
— Narrow brown ribbon
— Ruler
— Silver metal hanging rod (563216)
— Tape runner adhesive
— Wide pink ribbon

Directions

1. Cut the ivory cardstock to 5" x 9". Score and fold the cardstock in half to make a 5" x 4½" card. Cut a 5" x 2" strip of green patterned paper and adhere it to the top of the card's cover using tape runner adhesive. Cut a 5" x 2" strip of brown floral paper and glue it to the bottom of the cover.

2. Using craft glue, adhere the hanging rod to the die-cut oval frame to create a buckle. Use gel superglue to adhere jewels to the frame. Feed wide pink ribbon through the buckle to create a "belt," then use craft glue to adhere the belt to the center of the cover. Using brown ribbon, tie the "Mother's Day" tag to the buckle.

Nana Card

A one-of-a-kind grandmother deserves the special attention of a card made just for her. To enhance the card, try making or embellishing an envelope to match.

Materials

— Book text
— Brown shoe polish
— Clay-colored paper (MOT-062)
— Clean rag
— Craft glue
— Craft scissors
— Dimensional flower sticker (555099)
— Gold fabric
— Large alphabet stickers (553408)
— Mini brads
— Narrow rickrack
— Patterned paper (MOT-076)
— Ruler
— Tape runner adhesive
— Tiny tag

Directions

1. Cut the patterned paper to 8$\frac{1}{2}$" x 7". Use the rag and brown shoe polish to create thin, darkened lines on the paper. Score and fold the paper in half to make a 4$\frac{1}{4}$" x 7" card.

2. Cut the clay-colored paper to 8$\frac{1}{2}$" x 1$\frac{1}{4}$" and adhere it to the cover using tape runner adhesive. Apply the large alphabet stickers for "Nana" to the cover. Attach the mini brads to the ends of the clay-colored paper border. Adhere the rickrack to the bottom using craft glue.

3. Adhere a swatch of gold fabric to the card using craft glue. Apply a dimensional flower sticker to the card. Cut the letters L, O, V, and E from book text, then adhere them to the jewelry marking tag using tape runner adhesive. Tie the tag onto the dimensional sticker.

Dad's Day Card

Create a tool pegboard for this Father's Day card by punching a grid of holes into chipboard. Be sure to measure and mark the grid first so the holes are uniform.

Materials

— $1/8$" hole punch
— Black cardstock (631007)
— Black elastic cord
— Brads
— Brown inkpad
— Brown paper (48410)
— Chipboard
— Computer and printer
— Cotton ball or manicure pad
— Craft scissors
— Foam tape
— Hammer
— Hammer, pliers, and screwdriver embellishments (558397)
— Ivory acrylic paint
— Large alphabet stickers (553408)
— Large stencil-style alphabet stickers (553699)
— Measuring tape sticker (551565)
— Paintbrush
— Pencil
— Quote printed on ivory cardstock
— Ruler
— Screwdriver
— Stapler and staples
— Tape runner adhesive
— Tool-themed stickers (48005)

Directions

1. Cut the black cardstock to 10" x $6^1/2$". Score and fold it in half to make a 5" x $6^1/2$" card. Cut the brown paper to 5" x $6^1/2$" and adhere it to the cover using tape runner adhesive.

2. Cut the chipboard to $4^1/2$" x 6". Draw a grid with $1/2$" spaces on the chipboard. Use the hammer and $1/8$" punch to punch a hole through the chipboard at all the grid intersections.

3. Brush a wide stripe of ivory acrylic paint across the top of the "pegboard." Apply the measuring tape sticker across the width of the pegboard. Apply the D from the stencil-style alphabet over the painted stripe.

4. Age the edges of the stencil letter using brown ink and a cotton ball or manicure pad (see "Aging Paper," page 16). Complete the title by applying the A and D stickers from the large alphabet to the card.

5. Thread and stretch lengths of black elastic cord through the holes in the pegboard. Secure them by tying knots in the ends of the elastic at the back of the board. Place the pliers under one of these elastic holders.

6. Place the quote printed on ivory cardstock onto the pegboard with one end secured under the elastic holder and the other end stapled down. Slip the hammer and screwdriver embellishments and a tool-themed sticker under the elastic holder.

7. Place four brads at the corners of the pegboard and bend back the prongs to secure. Form "screws" from the brads by using a screwdriver and hammer to dent slots into the top of each brad. Attach the completed pegboard to the card with squares of foam tape.

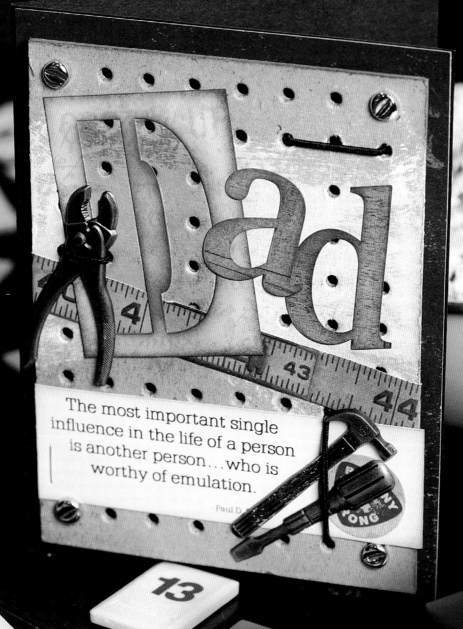

Dad

The most important single influence in the life of a person is another person…who is worthy of emulation.

- Paul D.

THINGS I LOVE ABOUT YOU

- Your happy disposition in the morning
- The way you care for your puppy
- HUGS! ...so tender
- That imagination - it blows me away!
- How you want to dress like Daddy on Saturdays.
- Really... there isn't anything that I don't ADORE about you.

Things I Love Tag

This one-of-a-kind design leaves plenty of room for you to remind the recipient just what it is about him that you love. I made this particular tag for my son. Hopefully, some day he will see it again and run to call his mother!

Materials

— 1/8" hole punch
— Black gingham paper (638488)
— Chipboard
— Craft glue
— Craft scissors
— Jumbo wooden craft sticks
— Jute
— Key charm (558151)
— Notebook paper
— Photograph
— Tape runner adhesive
— "Things I Love About You" sentiment (551756)
— Vintage-style script paper (639096)

Directions

1. Cut the chipboard to 3 1/4" x 7", rounding off the corners. Use tape runner adhesive to cover the tag with vintage-style script paper.

2. Handwrite a list onto notebook paper, then adhere it to the tag using tape runner adhesive. Use craft glue to adhere the key charm to the top of the tag. Punch holes at the top of the tag and tie the jute onto the tag and key. Use tape runner adhesive to adhere the photograph to the tag.

3. Trim the wooden craft sticks to the desired length. Using craft glue, cover the sticks with black gingham paper. Cut apart the sentiment, "Things I Love About You," and apply them to the sticks. *Note: You can stamp the words onto black paper instead.* Use tape runner adhesive to adhere the sticks to the tag.

Dreams Slide Mailer Card

Slide mailers are great for presenting photos or mini-books—just tuck the item into the little inset and you have both a card and gift wrap in one.

Materials

- ⅛" hole punch
- Black cardstock (631007)
- Black elastic cord
- Brick red acrylic paint
- Brown acrylic paint
- Computer and printer
- Craft scissors
- Dictionary-themed paper (636279)
- Distressed tag sticker (551558)
- "Dreams" label
- Fiber
- "Hope and Love" metal word plate (558045)
- Ivory cardstock (630918)
- Mini brads
- Paintbrush
- Photograph
- Slide mailer
- Small tag
- Tape measure-themed paper (636552)
- Tape runner adhesive
- Tiny text vellum (636460)
- Typewriter-style alphabet stickers (557031)

Directions

1. Cut the dictionary-themed paper into two pieces the size of the slide mailer. Adhere one piece to the cover and the other piece to the inside cover of the slide mailer using tape runner adhesive. Tear a piece of black cardstock and adhere it to the inside cover. Paint a brick red stripe along the top of the cover.

2. Cut a strip from the tape measure-themed paper. Fold over a portion of the left edge of the strip and secure the fold with two mini brads. Adhere the tape measure across the cover using tape runner adhesive and wrap it around to the inside. Trim the strip as necessary.

3. Add the "Dreams" label to the top of the tape measure on the cover. Type and print the words "Are Achieved Not in Miles, But in Inches" onto ivory cardstock. *Note: You can stamp the words onto strips of ivory cardstock instead.* Cut out the words and adhere them to the cover using tape runner adhesive.

4. Apply a distressed tag sticker to the inside cover. Use tape runner adhesive to adhere a torn rectangle of tiny text vellum and the photograph to the inside cover. Adhere a typewriter-style alphabet sticker to the inside cover.

5. Apply brick red paint to the slide mailer inset. Apply brown paint to the "Hope and Love" metal word plate. Punch holes in the top right and lower left corners of the inset. Thread a length of black elastic cord through the word plate then through the holes in the inset. Tie knots in the ends of the elastic at the back.

6. Using ivory cardstock, create a miniature card to fit inside the slide inset. Cut the tape measure-themed paper to the size of the miniature card and adhere it to the miniature card using tape runner adhesive. Tie a length of fiber at the fold of the miniature card and attach the small tag. Slide the completed miniature card into the inset under the elastic. Adhere the photograph to the vellum.

DREAMS

are achieved

not in miles,

but in inches.

Family Time

Friends Forever

When I think of my friends, I think of the memories we have created together and all that these valued people add to my life. Making thoughtfully crafted cards is my way of offering something beautiful to them. The friendship cards in this chapter are full of lovely colors, rich textures, and elegant details that make them a pleasure to make, give, and receive.

Girlfriend Card

A copper frame and embossed paper, along with fabric trim and ribbon, give dimension to this beautiful card. You can further personalize the card by placing a photo inside the frame.

Materials

— Craft glue
— Craft scissors
— Friendship-themed text paper (641198)
— Ribbon
— Rickrack
— Round copper frame (563438)
— Ruler
— Tape runner adhesive
— Vintage floral paper (641747)
— White flower trim

Directions

1. Cut the vintage floral paper to 10" x 7". Score and fold it in half to create a 5" x 7" card. Trim 1^1/$_2$" from the right side of the cover.

2. Cut friendship-themed text paper to 5" x 7". Use tape runner adhesive to line the inside of the card with the paper. Cut another piece of vintage floral paper to 3^1/$_2$" x 7". Line the inside of the cover with the paper.

3. Tie ribbons and rickrack to one-third of the round copper frame. Use craft glue to adhere the frame to the top-right edge of the cover.

4. Cut out the word or letters for "Girlfriend" from the friendship-themed text paper. Use tape runner adhesive to adhere to the cover. Use craft glue to adhere rickrack and white flower trim as desired to the cover.

Friends Forever

Friends Forever Card

To easily add a homespun, textural element to a card, look for transfers, stickers, and tapes that recall the appearance of hand-sewn details.

Materials

- 2" circle template
- Blue-gray patterned paper (MOT-072)
- Book text
- Clear dimensional adhesive
- Corner rounder (optional)
- Craft knife
- Craft scissors
- Domed alphabet stickers (545007)
- "Friends" dimensional sticker (555105)
- Ivory acrylic paint
- Jade-green patterned paper (MOT-070)
- Paintbrush
- Pencil
- Pistachio-green paper (ACS-044)
- Ribbons
- Ruler
- Stitches transfer (590151)
- Tape runner adhesive

Directions

1. Cut the pistachio-green paper to 5" x 7". Score and fold the paper in half to create a 5" x 3^1/$_2$" card. Cut blue-gray patterned paper to 5" x 1^1/$_2$". Score and fold the blue-gray paper strip in half lengthwise. Use tape runner adhesive to adhere the strip to the bottom of the card, wrapping it around the edge to the inside cover. Round the bottom corners of the card.

2. Trace the circle template onto the cover. Use the craft knife to cut out the circle (see "Cutting Out Windows," page 17). Wrap three ribbons through this hole and around the right edge of the card. Tie each ribbon in a knot, staggering the placement of the knots. Apply the stitches transfer to the bottom edge of the cover.

3. Cut the jade-green patterned paper to 4^3/$_4$" x 3^1/$_4$". Round the bottom edges. Use tape runner adhesive to adhere the paper to the inside of the card. Cut the blue-gray patterned paper to 1^1/$_2$" x 3^1/$_4$" and adhere it to the inside. Apply the "Friends" dimensional sticker to the inside, making certain that it appears inside the 2" circle cut from the cover when the card is closed.

4. To complete the message on the interior of the card, apply domed alphabet stickers for "Forever" to book text using clear dimensional adhesive. Adhere the book text around the "Friends" dimensional sticker using tape runner adhesive.

Friends Forever

Purse Gift Card Enclosure

The presentation of a gift card or certificate can be just as much fun as the gift itself. Use this cute purse design the next time you want to treat a friend to a shopping spree.

Materials

- ¼" hole punch
- 18-gauge wire
- Blue daisies paper (660809)
- Clear stretch beading cord
- Craft scissors
- Craft glue
- Glass beads
- Large floral print paper (660793)
- Pink flower dimensional sticker (555679)
- Pink pompom trim
- Plain, tag-shaped card (240063)
- Ruler
- Small colored frames (563599)
- Tape runner adhesive
- Wire cutters

Directions

1. Trim 2" from the bottom of the plain, tag-shaped card cover. Cut the large floral print paper to 5" x 4" and use tape runner adhesive to adhere it to the cover, aligning the bottom and side edges. Cut the blue daisies paper to 5" x 2½" and adhere it to the top half of the card, leaving ½" of the bottom edge unattached. Trim the top corners to fit the card.

2. Use craft glue to adhere pink pompom trim to the card, tucking the top edge under the blue daisies paper. Apply the pink flower dimensional sticker to the cover. Thread a length of clear stretch beading cord through the small hole in the small colored frame. *Note: If your frame doesn't have a hole in it, make one with an awl.* Tie the frame to the middle of the length of beading cord. Wrap the ends of the cord around the top foam layer of the dimensional sticker. Tie the frame to the foam layer.

3. Score the inside of the card from left to right, 1" from the top. Adhere the front and back of the card together above the score mark.

4. Punch two holes at the top of the card. Run one end of the wire through a hole. Wrap the end up and around itself to secure. Thread glass beads onto the wire to the desired length of the handle. Trim the wire and secure it to the second hole in the card in the same manner as the opposite hole.

5. Cut the blue daisies paper to 5" x 3½". Adhere it to the inside of the card using tape runner adhesive and aligning at the top and side edges. Score and fold up 2" of the back cover's bottom edge to the inside. Create a pocket for the gift card enclosure by adhering the sides of this fold to the card. Cut the large floral print paper to 5" x 2" and adhere it to the front of the pocket.

Friends Forever

Laugh Card

Ball motifs and rolling text give this card a lighthearted feel. This is a great pick-me-up for those times when a good friend needs a lift.

Materials

— ⅛" hole punch
— Book text
— Brad (564275)
— Circle-patterned paper (ACS-056)
— Craft scissors
— Jump rings
— Large circle tag (ACS-026)
— "Laugh" sticker (551145)
— Ribbon
— Ruler
— Shipping tag (ACS-026)
— Small circle tags (ACS-026)
— Striped paper (ACS-060)
— Tape runner adhesive

Directions

1. Cut the striped paper to 4¾" x 10". Score and fold the paper in half to make a 4¾" x 5" card. Trim 1½" from the bottom edge of the cover.

2. Cut the circle-patterned paper to 4¾" x 5". Using tape runner adhesive, adhere it to the inside of the card then apply the "Laugh" sticker to the bottom of the circle-patterned paper.

3. Adhere one large and two small circle tags to the cover, placing the holes of the small circle tags outside the edges of the card and the hole of the large circle tag near the top of the card so that the tag to be added later will hide it. Trim the small tags so that the tag edges are flush with the card edges.

4. Cut out "ha ha" and "tee hee" several times from book text. *Note: You can use a computer to type and print out the text instead.* Adhere each letter in a swooping fashion from left to right, up and over the circle tags.

5. Handwrite a quote onto a shipping tag. Attach a brad to the hole in the tag. Adhere the tag to the cover. Punch two holes at the top of the tag. Attach a jump ring to each hole. Tie ribbon onto each jump ring.

Friends Forever

Good Friends Tag

A flower-shaped sun catcher moves from capturing light at a window to give this tag color and cheer. If you wish, you can give the flowers even more dimension by filling in the sections with crystal lacquer.

Materials

— Acrylic paints
— Craft glue
— Craft scissors
— Domes floral buttons (557925)
— Embroidery floss
— "Good Friends Are Everywhere" dimensional sticker (555730)
— Floral-and-striped paper (639508)
— Foam tape
— Ivory cardstock (630918)
— Paintbrush
— Plastic flower-shaped sun catcher
— Ribbons
— Ruler
— Tape runner adhesive

Directions

1. Cut a 4$\frac{1}{2}$" x 6$\frac{1}{4}$" tag from ivory cardstock. Cut the floral-and-striped paper to 4$\frac{1}{2}$" x 6$\frac{1}{4}$" and adhere to the tag using tape runner adhesive.

2. Paint the flower-shaped sun catcher with acrylic paints.

3. Thread embroidery floss through a domed floral button and tie in a bow. Repeat for the remaining buttons. Adhere the buttons to the centers of the flowers using craft glue.

4. Tie ribbons to the sun catcher hole. Attach the flowers to the tag with foam tape.

5. Apply the "Good Friends Are Everywhere" dimensional sticker to the tag.

Friends Forever

Life Is Beautiful Card

The flower on this design is made by threading ribbon through holes in a circle string clasp and looping it to make the petals. Narrow strips of fabric can be used in place of the ribbon for a different look.

Materials

- ½"-wide grosgrain ribbon in green, pink, and yellow
- ½"-wide magenta ribbon
- ⅛" hole punch
- Adhesive foam dot
- Black marker
- Craft glue
- Craft scissors
- Green floral paper (639638)
- Green felt
- Green string
- "Life Is Beautiful" dimensional sticker (555730)
- Pink bead
- Pink-with-white-dots paper (639447)
- Plain card with top flap (240162)
- Ruler
- Stapler and staples
- String clasp (542662)
- Striped paper (639546)
- Tape runner adhesive

Directions

1. Cut the pink-with-white-dots paper to the size of the plain card's flap. Adhere the paper to the front of the flap using tape runner adhesive. Cut the green floral paper to the size of the cover. Adhere the paper to the cover.

2. Cut the striped paper to 4¼" x 1½". Fold and staple the green, pink, and yellow ribbons to the paper, then adhere the paper to the card using tape runner adhesive.

3. To make the flower, punch eight holes around the string clasp. Starting underneath the clasp, thread magenta ribbon through one hole, loop to the back and thread the ribbon up through the adjacent hole. Continue in this fashion until all the petals are formed. Trim the ribbon ends and adhere to the back of the string clasp with craft glue. Adhere the flower to the card flap with an adhesive foam dot.

4. Thread a pink bead onto a length of green string. Center it on the string and tie it in place. Cut two leaves from green felt. Make a small slit in the top leaf and push the bead up through it. Glue the two leaves together, making certain that the green string is coming out the base of the leaf. Tie the opposite end of the string around the flower. Wrap the string around the card and encircle the flower for a clasp.

5. Apply the "Life Is Beautiful" dimensional sticker to the card. Draw spots on the bead with black marker to create a ladybug.

life is bEautiFul!

Friends Forever

LIVE
life
in the
direction
it takes
you

Party

JUST MOVED

WHO
WHAT
WHEN
where

David & Maddie Carson

Pull up a box and relax.

We're taking a break from moving

to have some fun.

September 20th

1705 Lakeview Pointe

Kansas City

Dr. T.A. Brown
4216 Ridgeline Dr.
Newbold, OR 87481

WE HAVE **MOVED**

JOURNEY

New Beginnings

Beginnings can be exciting and full of hope, but crossing a new threshold can also be a bit scary. Sharing a sentiment with friends, family members, or neighbors during times of transition is a way of showing your support and giving them the warmth and familiarity of something handmade.

New Beginnings Card

Rub-on transfers are an easy way to add titles or sentiments. They can be applied over photos, acetate, ribbon, fabric, glass, or metal. You can choose to use a transfer as-is or create new words by carefully cutting the letters apart before applying them.

Materials

— Blue daisies paper (660809)
— Colored frame with chain (564695)
— Craft glue
— Craft scissors
— Ivory cardstock (630918)
— Lime-green-with-dots paper (660700)
— "New Beginnings" transfer (590045)
— Paisley paper (660908)
— Pinking shears
— Ribbon
— Ruler
— Stitches transfer (590151)
— Tape runner adhesive

Directions

1. Cut the ivory cardstock to 8" x 7". Score and fold it in half to make a 4" x 7" card. Cut the paisley paper to 4" x 7" and adhere to the cover using tape runner adhesive.

2. Cut the blue daisies paper to 2" x 7". Trim the right side with pinking shears. Adhere the paper to the cover of the card using tape runner adhesive. Apply the stitches transfer along the trimmed edge.

3. Thread a length of ribbon through the chain of the colored frame. Use craft glue to adhere the ribbon to the card.

4. Cut the lime-green-with-dots paper to $1\frac{1}{4}$" x 7" and use tape runner adhesive to adhere to the card over the blue daisies paper.

5. Apply the "New Beginnings" transfer to the card over the lime-green-with-dots paper.

NEW BEGINNINGS

New Beginnings

good things are going to happen

you're in my heart

Good Things Card

Sometimes a design element gets lost in the background. To make it pop out, like the flower stickers on this card, try incorporating dimension with foam tape. The effect is fun, full of energy, and perfect for celebrating the good things in life.

Materials

- Blue floral paper (639553)
- Craft knife
- Craft scissors
- Embossed flower stickers (551985)
- Flower embossed glitter sticker (551985)
- Foam tape
- Green-and-yellow-striped paper (639423)
- "Good Things Are Going to Happen" sticker (551985)
- Ivory cardstock (630918)
- Plain card with scalloped window (240032)
- Ruler
- Tape runner adhesive
- "You're In My Heart" sticker (551978)

Directions

1. Cut the blue floral paper to 5" x 7". Using the window of the plain card as a template, cut a 2$\frac{1}{2}$" square from the center of the blue floral piece (see "Cutting Out Windows," page 17). Adhere the 5" x 7" paper to the cover using tape runner adhesive.

2. Cut a 5" x 2" piece from the green-and-yellow-striped paper and use tape runner adhesive to adhere it to the bottom of the cover, creating a border.

3. Apply the "You're In My Heart" sticker to the card. Apply a few embossed flower stickers along the top of the striped border, leaving spaces between them. To add dimension to some of the flower stickers, apply them to cardstock, cut them out, and fill the spaces along the top of the border by adhering them to the card using foam tape.

4. Cut a 5" x 7" piece from the green-and-yellow-striped paper and adhere it to the inside of the card. Apply the embossed medallion sticker to cardstock and cut it out. Using foam tape, adhere the embossed medallion sticker to the inside of the card, centered inside the window.

5. Apply the "Good Things Are Going To Happen" sticker to a piece of cardstock. Cut it out and adhere it to the top front of the card with foam tape.

New Beginnings

Live Tag

Inspired by the quote on the front, this design uses a freely spinning arrow and a suitcase motif to reflect the theme of letting yourself flow into the new challenges and adventures that life presents.

Materials

— Black marker
— Craft scissors
— Embossed flower sticker (551428)
— Foam tape
— Green textured paper (660380)
— Ivory cardstock (630918)
— Large alphabet stickers (553620)
— Pearl brad (563247)
— Polka-dotted paper (660311)
— Ruler
— Spinner
— Tape runner adhesive
— Yellow textured paper (660373)

Directions

1. Cut ivory cardstock to 5" x 8". Apply the C from the large alphabet stickers to the top of the cardstock, making certain the ends of the C stick to the edge of the cardstock, with the curve of the C extending upward. Adhere a second C to the back of the first C. Cut the polka-dotted paper to 5" x 8" and adhere to the tag using tape runner adhesive.

2. Write the words "life in the direction it takes you" onto the green textured paper and trim the paper to 2^1/2" x 8". Adhere to the tag using tape runner adhesive. Apply the large alphabet stickers to the yellow textured paper to spell "Live." Cut out each letter in a block then adhere the letters to the tag.

3. Apply an embossed flower sticker to cardstock then cut out around the flower. Place the prongs from the pearl brad through the spinner, the embossed flower sticker, a piece of foam tape, and then the tag. Bend back the prongs to secure.

Moving Party Card

What better time to throw a party than when you need a break from packing to relax with friends? Rip pieces of cardboard from the multitude of boxes that surround you to create these invitations.

Materials

— Black label-style alphabet stickers (667099)
— Black marker
— Cardboard
— Clay-brown paper (MOT-062)
— Craft scissors
— Large alphabet stickers (553408)
— Round metal-rimmed tag (564336)
— Ruler
— String
— Tape runner adhesive
— "Who," "What," "When," and "Where" dimensional stickers (555143)

Directions

1. Cut the cardboard to 4³/4" x 7". Cut the clay-brown paper to 4¹/4" x 5¹/2". Round the corners of the paper and adhere to the cardboard using tape runner adhesive.

2. Apply black label-style alphabet stickers for "Just Moved" to the metal-rimmed tag. Wrap string around the card, place the tag onto the string, and tie the string in a knot.

3. Apply large alphabet stickers for "Party" to the card. Apply the "Who," "What," "When," and "Where" dimensional stickers down the side of the card. Use the black marker to write in the party information.

New Beginnings

We Have Moved Card

Moving notices remind friends that you want to stay in touch. In this design, the recipient pulls on the "Journey" label to view a tag on which you have written your new address.

Materials

— Architecture-themed paper (638709)
— Black label-style alphabet stickers (667099)
— Cardboard
— Craft scissors
— Floral fabric textured paper (610491)
— Ivory cardstock (630918)
— "Journey" file tab (550360)
— Large alphabet stickers (553569)
— Map-themed acetate (639133)
— Marker
— Ochre textured paper (MOT-065)
— Pinking shears
— Postage-stamp sticker (553569)
— Ruler
— Stapler and staples
— Tape runner adhesive

Directions

1. Cut cardboard to 7" x 4$\frac{1}{2}$". Staple a 6$\frac{1}{2}$" x 4$\frac{1}{2}$" piece of map-themed acetate to the cardboard along the top and bottom edges. *Note: Leave the sides open so that a tag can slide from the right side.*

2. Cut the architecture-themed paper to 4$\frac{1}{2}$" x 3$\frac{3}{4}$" and adhere it to the card using tape runner adhesive. Cut a 3$\frac{3}{4}$" square from the floral fabric textured paper using pinking shears. Cut a 3$\frac{1}{2}$" x 1$\frac{1}{2}$" strip of ivory cardstock. Score and fold the ivory cardstock. Staple the cardstock to the top edge of the fabric textured paper to create a swatch. Adhere the swatch to the card.

3. Apply the large alphabet stickers for "Moved" and the postage-stamp sticker to the card. *Note: The alphabet stickers I used have decorative background, but you can also apply stickers to scraps of different decorative papers and adhere them to the card using tape runner adhesive.*

4. Cut a 6" x 2" tag from the ochre textured paper. Write the new contact information on the tag with the marker. Attach the "Journey" file tab to the right edge. Insert the tag under the acetate from the right side of the card.

HAMILTON
FOOD CO.

sugar
&spice
and everything nice!

congratulations
on the birth
of your baby

Baby
Boy

ABCDEFGHI   ABCDEFGHI
POINT

A BABY IS

LO
VE

TINY TOT
SHO

baby

Little
Princess

Just Arrived

A baby card is, of course, not really for the baby. It's for the parents—to congratulate them on an exciting event and to share in their joy. Giving something lovingly made to new parents is a wonderful gesture to show them how important their new arrival is to you.

A Baby is Love Gift Card Enclosure

Want to present a gift card in style? This dimensional design holds a card in a plastic sleeve that slides through a slit at the top of the enclosure for a dramatic presentation, but folds flat for easy mailing.

Materials

— Black inkpad
— Book text
— Buttons
— Craft glue
— Craft knife
— Craft scissors
— Dot-patterned embossed paper (660946)
— "Love" dimensional sticker (555952)
— Patterned acetate (660991)
— Pink tulle
— Ruler
— Scalloped scissors
— Striped paper (660762)
— Tape runner adhesive
— Top-loading trading card sleeve
— Wings stamp (Inkadinkado 8367 X)

Directions

1. Cut the dot-patterned embossed paper to 4" x 12". Score and fold it in half, matching the short edges. Unfold. Score and fold in each short edge ½". Fold these two ends into the middle fold line and crease. Unfold.

2. Use the craft knife to make a 3" slit along the middle fold line, leaving ½" uncut on either side of the slit.

3. Refold the ½" short edges. Refold the paper in half, matching the folded short edges. Lay the trading card sleeve inside the folded piece, with the closed end of the sleeve sandwiched between the two ½" short edges and aligned at the bottom edges. Use craft glue to adhere the trading card sleeve to the right sides of these flaps, making certain that the top of the sleeve is lined up with the 3" slit. *Note: When the top of the card is pushed down, the trading card sleeve will pop up through the slit.*

4. Using scalloped scissors, cut a 4" x 2" strip from the striped paper. Adhere to the top of the card using tape runner adhesive.

5. Stamp the wings onto patterned acetate with black ink. Roughly cut outside the lines of the wings. Layer and adhere with craft glue two pieces of pink tulle, the acetate wings, and the "Love" dimensional sticker to the card. Cut the letters to spell "A Baby Is" from book text. Use tape runner adhesive to adhere the letters to the card. Use craft glue to adhere buttons down the left side of the card.

(Inset, right) When the top of the box-like card is pushed down, a trading card sleeve—holding a gift card or certificate—comes up through the slit.

Gift Card or Certificate

Just Arrived

Baby Shower Card

Remember texture when you are trying to convey a feeling. Soft felt, made to resemble a towel, fits the gently playful theme of this card.

Materials

— Blue-with-white-dots card (253032)

— Craft glue

— Craft scissors

— Domed alphabet stickers (560109)

— Duck dimensional sticker (555990)

— Embossed alphabet stickers (270022)

— Felt

— Needle and thread

— Pinking shears

— Ruler

— Tape runner adhesive

— Yellow gingham card (253032)

Directions

1. Cut a $2^3/4$" x $5^1/4$" piece from felt. Trim the bottom of the felt with pinking shears. Stitch across the felt 2" from the bottom and again $3/4$" from the bottom. Make $1/2$" snips along the bottom of the felt for fringe. Use craft glue to adhere the towel to the yellow gingham card.

2. Apply the embossed alphabet stickers for "Baby" to the blue-with-white-dots card. Cut out each letter in a block and adhere it to the yellow gingham card using tape runner adhesive. Apply the duck dimensional sticker and the domed alphabet stickers for "Shower" to the card.

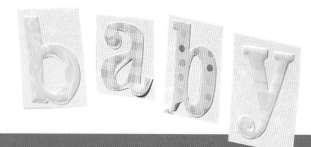

Sugar & Spice Card

Warm cinnamon and sweet pink colors reflect the sentiment of this pretty card. The look of the metal charms is softened with an application of ivory paint.

Materials

— Baby buggy charm (558762)

— Craft scissors

— Dark dot-patterned paper (660885)

— Embossed dot-patterned paper (660946)

— Ivory acrylic paint

— Ivory trim

— Jump ring

— Lime-green dotted paper (660700)

— Needle and thread

— Paintbrush

— Pink patterned paper (660748)

— Plain Card (240155)

— Ribbon

— Ruler

— Safety pin

— "Sugar & Spice and Everything Nice" patch (580398)

— Tape runner adhesive

Directions

1. Cut the pink patterned paper to the size of the plain card cover and adhere it to the cover using tape runner adhesive. Cut the embossed dot-patterned paper to 4" x 4$\frac{1}{4}$" and adhere it to the cover. Cut or tear the lime-green dotted paper and the dark dot-patterned paper to 2$\frac{1}{2}$" x 3". Stitch each piece of paper to the cover.

2. Adhere the ivory trim and the "Sugar & Spice and Everything Nice" patch to the cover using tape runner adhesive.

3. Paint the baby buggy charm with ivory acrylic paint. Place a jump ring on the charm and attach it to the card with a safety pin. Tie a length of ribbon to the safety pin.

Just Arrived

Baby Boy Card

The dimensional sticker used in this design doubles as an embellishment and as a post for wrapping the cord closure.

Materials

— "Baby Boy" dimensional sticker (555891)

— Bead

— Blue striped card (259010)

— "Congratulations on the Birth of Your Baby" transfer (290037)

— Cord

— Craft scissors

— Felt

— Green quilted "Baby" paper (642300)

— Ruler

— Scalloped scissors

— Tape runner adhesive

Directions

1. Cut the green quilted "Baby" paper to 4¹/₄" x 3¹/₄". Trim the bottom with scalloped scissors. Adhere the paper to the blue striped card with tape runner adhesive.

2. Apply the "Baby Boy" dimensional sticker to the card. Tie one end of the cord around the sticker. Thread a bead onto the other end of the cord and tie the end into a knot. Wrap the cord around the card and encircle the sticker for a closure. Cut the felt into strips and tie the strips to the cord. Apply the "Congratulations on the Birth of Your Baby" transfer onto the card.

Little Princess Card

The tiny hair clip on this card holds embellishments in place while emphasizing the diva attitude created by feathers and glittering gems.

Materials

— Diamond-patterned card (259010)

— Foam tape

— Gel superglue

— Green tag (257030)

— Hair clip

— Jewels

— "Little Princess" dimensional sticker (555884)

— Pink feathers

— Ribbon

— Sandpaper

Directions

1. Sand the edges of the green tag. Apply the "Little Princess" dimensional sticker to the tag. Adhere the jewels to the tag using gel superglue.

2. Tie ribbon to the tag hole. Adhere the tag to the diamond-patterned card with foam tape. Attach the pink feathers and tag ribbon ends to the top of the card with the hair clip.

Just Arrived

Happy, Happy Birthday

Each year, we get a whole day to ourselves; a day to treat ourselves to our favorite things, to laugh and have fun; a day where we get free license to simply enjoy ourselves. Birthday cards should add to the fun and joy of someone's special day. The cards in this chapter will do just that with cheerful words, phrases, and designs.

Celebrate Card

Textured metal frames adorned with bows pose as birthday presents on this colorful card. You can add a fun detail by hanging a tiny tag with the recipient's name on it from the top package. Allow the tag to dangle inside the card's window.

Materials

— Alphabet stamps (Inkadinkado 94146)
— Black inkpad
— Colored frames in green, pink, and yellow (564053)
— Craft knife
— Craft scissors
— Green-and-pink patterned paper (639591)
— Green and pink ribbons
— Green paper (639454)
— Pink cardstock
— Ruler
— Tape runner adhesive
— Yellow floral paper (639591)

Directions

1. Cut the pink cardstock to 10" x 7". Score and fold it in half to make a 5" x 7" card. Cut a piece from the yellow floral paper to be slightly smaller than the card cover then adhere the paper to the cover using tape runner adhesive. *Note: The yellow floral paper I used already had a green scalloped border that I positioned at the bottom of the card, but you can create one from green paper and adhere it separately.*

2. Cut two pieces from the green-and-pink patterned paper to fit behind the green frame and yellow frame. Adhere the frames to the paper. Tie ribbons around the two frames. Adhere these two "packages" to the card.

3. Using the inside of the pink frame as a template, cut a window out of the cover with a craft knife (see "Cutting Out Windows," page 17). Tie a ribbon to the pink frame and adhere to the card over the window.

4. Stamp "Celebrate" onto green paper with black ink. Cut out the letters in blocks and adhere them to the front of the card using tape runner adhesive.

5. To finish the interior of the card, cut a scalloped border from green-and-pink patterned paper. Trim the border to fit inside the card, making certain the green shows through the window when the card is closed.

CELEBRATE

Happy, Happy Birthday

Party Hat Card

I normally use pages from an old book as a source for text, but here it serves as decorative fringe on a playful party hat.

Materials

- 1½" circle punch
- Craft glue
- Craft scissors
- Cream-and-teal-striped paper (639652)
- Felt trim
- Flower embellishments (580145)
- Foam tape
- Ivory cardstock (630918)
- Old book pages
- Party hat pattern (page 140)
- Pencil
- Ruler
- Scalloped scissors
- Tape runner adhesive
- Teal floral paper (639492)

Directions

1. Trace the party hat pattern onto the ivory cardstock and teal floral paper and cut out. Adhere the teal floral paper to the cardstock using tape runner adhesive.

2. Cut a stripe from the cream-and-teal-striped paper using scalloped scissors. Adhere the stripe down the center of the hat then trim the edges to fit the card.

3. Cut pages from the old book into five 1¼" x 1½" rectangles. Adhere the rectangles to the bottom of the hat, overlapping them slightly and extending them ½" past the edge. Cut slits at the bottom of the rectangles to create fringe.

4. Punch two 1½" circles from ivory cardstock and two from book text. Adhere each book text circle to each cardstock circle. Cut slits around each circle. With right sides facing up, attach the circles together with foam tape. Use tape runner adhesive to adhere the circles to the top of the hat. Use craft glue to adhere the flower embellishments and felt trim to the hat.

Happy, Happy Birthday

Birthday Bracelet Card

Some brads are too much fun to use only in the standard way. When I first saw the ones I used for this card, I couldn't resist a creative challenge. With a few twists of the prongs, the bracelet component of this project was born.

Materials

- Beads
- "Birthday Joy" sticker (551152)
- Button-topped brads (250093)
- Cable chain
- Chipboard
- Circular tag (ACS-026)
- Clear domed stickers (557413)
- Craft scissors
- Foam tape
- "For You" transfer (590113)
- Headpins
- Heart charms (564176)
- Ivory cardstock (630918)
- Jewelry bag pattern (page 139)
- Lobster clasp
- Needle-nosed pliers
- Patterned paper (ACS-055)
- Pencil
- Ribbon
- Ruler
- Split rings
- Square-topped decorative brads (564282)
- Tape runner adhesive

Card Directions

1. Trace the jewelry bag pattern onto the patternedpaper three times, making certain one of the traced shapes is in reverse. Trace the pattern onto chipboard once. Cut out each piece. To create the card, use tape runner adhesive to adhere the reverse patterned paper piece onto the back of the chipboard and one of the remaining patterned pieces onto the front.

2. Score the third patterned paper piece horizontally 2½" from the bottom edge. Turn the piece over and place adhesive onto the paper above the score mark. Adhere to the covered chipboard piece.

3. Cut the "Birthday Joy" sticker into two pieces. Apply each piece to ivory cardstock and cut out. Adhere each piece to the jewelry bag with foam tape.

4. Apply the "For You" transfer to the circular tag. Place a ribbon around the neck of the bag, thread the tag onto the ribbon, and tie the ribbon in a bow.

Bracelet Directions

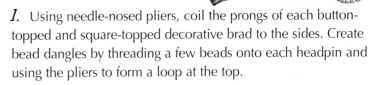

1. Using needle-nosed pliers, coil the prongs of each button-topped and square-topped decorative brad to the sides. Create bead dangles by threading a few beads onto each headpin and using the pliers to form a loop at the top.

2. Use a split ring to connect one button-topped brad to one square-topped brad while also attaching a bead dangle or a heart charm. Repeat until the bracelet is the desired length. Attach a lobster clasp to one end and a 1½" length of cable chain to the opposite end.

3. Apply a clear domed sticker to the back of each brad. Wrap the finished bracelet around the card and close the clasp at the back.

Happy, Happy Birthday

MAY ALL YOUR dreAms COME TRUE

celebrate 30

May Your Dreams Come True Card

The ruffled trim "frosting" and the ribbon "candles" for this birthday cake card were originally clean and white. A light coat of brown ink made them match the vintage look of the paper products.

Materials

- Brown Ink
- "Celebrate" domed sticker (545038)
- Cotton ball or manicure pad
- Corner rounder (optional)
- Craft glue
- Craft scissors
- Embossed circle-patterned paper (641754)
- Jade-green textured paper (MOT-063)
- "May All Your Dreams Come True" dimensional sticker (555129)
- Number stickers (ACS-027)
- Rectangle hole punch
- Ribbons
- Ruffled trim
- Ruler
- String
- Tag die-cut (ACS-026)
- Tape runner adhesive
- Yellow textured paper (ACS-046)

Directions

1. Cut the embossed circle-patterned paper into two 4"x 5" pieces. Round all the corners.

2. Score a 4" x 5" piece horizontally ³/₄" from the top. Turn the piece over and place tape runner adhesive onto the paper above the score line. Align the paper on top of the remaining piece of paper and adhere them together. Lift back the top piece of paper to lightly crease the score line.

3. Age the ribbons and ruffled trim using brown ink and a cotton ball or manicure pad (see "Aging Paper, page 16). Punch rectangular holes at the top of the card and tie ribbons through each hole. Use craft glue to adhere ruffled trim to the card below the score line. Use craft glue to adhere the "May All Your Dreams Come True" dimensional sticker to the center of the trim.

4. Decorate the tag die-cut with the number and "Celebrate" stickers. Tie the tag die-cut to the dimensional sticker with string. Secure the tag die-cut to the card with foam tape.

5. Cut the jade-green textured paper into two 5" x 2" pieces. Match the wrong sides and adhere them together with tape runner adhesive. Round the corners. Adhere to the inside of the card, allowing ¹/₂" to extend past the bottom and side edges.

6. Cut the yellow textured paper to 4" x 4". Round the two bottom corners and adhere to the inside of the card using tape runner adhesive.

Happy, Happy Birthday

Happy Birthday to You Card

The triangular flaps of an unusual plain card inspired this design. To reflect the shape they create when the card is closed, I stamped a diamond background. The round medallion stamp across the closure further unifies the overall look.

Materials

— Book text
— Brown inkpad
— Beads
— Craft scissors
— Diamond stamp (Inkadinkado 90338)
— Foam tape
— "Happy" and "Birthday" dimensional stickers (555143)
— Jade-green paper (MOT-063)
— Jade-green patterned paper (MOT-070)
— Medallion stamp (Inkadinkado 90657)
— Old book text
— Plain card with pointed flaps (240186)
— Ruler
— String
— Tape runner adhesive

Directions

1. Cut the jade-green patterned paper into two piecesthe size of the plain card's pointed flaps. Use tape runner adhesive to adhere the paper to the flaps.

2. Cut the jade-green paper to 4" x 5½". Stamp the diamonds onto the paper using brown ink. Cut the paper in half to form two 2" x 5½" pieces. Adhere one piece to each card panel under the pointed flaps. Stamp the medallion in the center of the card across the opening with brown ink. Secure the pointed flaps down with foam tape.

3. Apply the "Happy" and "Birthday" dimensional stickers to each side of the card opening. Create a closure for the card by tying string around the "Happy" dimensional sticker. Wind the string around both dimensional stickers in a figure-eight fashion. Tie a knot approximately 2" from the end of the string then thread beads onto the 2" end. Tie a second knot to secure the beads

4. Cut the letters for "To You" from book text. Use tape runner adhesive to adhere the words under the "Birthday" sticker.

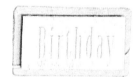

Happy, Happy Birthday

Make a Wish Card

The retro feel of this card comes from the circle dangles, which are reminiscent of layers of shiny sequins.

Materials

— ⅛" hole punch
— Brown floral paper (661158)
— Circle punches in three sizes
— Craft scissors
— Diamond-patterned paper (661110)
— Gel superglue
— Green floral paper (661134)
— Ivory cardstock (630918)
— Jewels
— Large jump rings
— "Make a Wish" transfer (590090)
— Pink floral paper (661127)
— Ruler
— Tape runner adhesive

Directions

1. Cut the ivory cardstock to 8" x 7". Score and fold it in half to create a 4" x 7" card.

2. Cut the pink floral paper to 4" x 7" and adhere it to the cover using tape runner adhesive. Cut the diamond-patterned paper to 2" x 7" and adhere it to the left side of the cover.

3. Cut the brown floral paper to 4" x 2½". Punch three evenly spaced ⅛" holes at the bottom of the paper then adhere the paper to the cover. *Note: You will be adhering jump rings to these holes, so make certain not to place adhesive on the area around each hole.*

4. Punch three small circles from the pink floral paper, three medium circles from the brown floral paper, and three large circles from the green floral paper. Align the tops of the circles and punch a ⅛" hole through each set. Attach the circle sets to the brown floral paper with jump rings (see "Attaching Jump Rings," page 16).

5. Apply the "Make a Wish!" transfer to the cover. Use gel superglue to adhere jewels to the cover.

Happy, Happy Birthday

Enjoy Card

Instead of having an embellishment compete for attention with a large title, I decided to place one over the O of this card's title to enhance the letter.

Materials

— Black ink
— Brown shoe polish
— Clean rag
— Craft glue
— Craft scissors
— Date stamp
— Embossed floral paper (641211)
— Faded red paper (ACS-045)
— Foam tape
— Large alphabet stickers (553637)
— Patterned paper (ACS-049)
— Rectangular label frame (564343)
— Ribbon
— Ruler
— Sewing machine and thread
— Small calendar sheet
— Tape runner adhesive
— "What Makes You Laugh" transfer (590137)
— Wooden nickel (580473)

Directions

1. Cut the embossed floral paper to 6³/₄" x 5". Cut a semicircle from the right side of the paper.

2. Age the large alphabet stickers for "Enjoy" using brown shoe polish and a clean rag before removing them from their backing (see "Aging Paper," page 16). Adhere the letters to the cover. Apply the "What makes you laugh" transfer across the card.

3. Cut the patterned paper to 7" x 5". Match the wrong sides of the patterned paper and the embossed floral paper, aligning the left sides. Sew the front and back of the card together at three edges, leaving the right side open for the pocket.

4. Stamp the recipient's birth date inside the O using black ink. Use foam tape to attach the rectangular label frame to the O. Wrap a length of ribbon around the card vertically and tie each end to the frame.

5. Cut a 6" x 4" tag from the faded red paper. Adhere the calendar sheet to the tag using tape runner adhesive. Adhere the wooden nickel to the tag using craft glue. Slide the tag into the card pocket.

Happy, Happy Birthday

Trick or Treat

The dusky autumn colors and the vintage, almost folk-art look of harvest motifs make the process of creating cards and tags for Halloween exceptionally fun. The projects in this chapter range from party invitations to greeting cards and goody-bag tags that will help everyone get in the spooky spirit.

Halloween Treat Bag Tag

Plastic spiders and special dimensional stickers add depth to this tag. To personalize this design, try tying a small label with the recipient's name around the cat's neck.

Materials

— Black marker
— Black-with-beige-dots paper (660670)
— Candy wrappers
— Cat dimensional sticker (555846)
— Craft glue
— Craft scissors
— Felt trim
— Green-striped card (259010)
— Pinking shears
— Plastic spiders
— Ruler
— Tape runner adhesive
— "Trick-or-Treat" dimensional sticker (555846)

Directions

1. Create a tag by cutting the green-striped card in half along the scored line. Trim the top of the tag with pinking shears. Cut the black-with-beige-dots paper to $4^1/4''$ x $1^1/2''$ and adhere it to the bottom of the tag using tape runner adhesive.

2. Apply the cat and "Trick-or-Treat" dimensional stickers to the tag. Form a handle by gluing the ends of the felt trim to the back of the tag. Using craft glue, adhere candy wrappers to the back of the tag then adhere plastic spiders to the cover. Draw spiderwebs on the cover with the black marker.

Trick or Treat

Halloween Pumpkin Card

This card opens from a hinge instead of a traditional fold. You can use various hinges to attach the cover to the card base, such as ribbons, strings, jump rings, metal hinges, fabric strips, or twist ties.

Materials

- ⅛" hole punch
- 1" circle punch
- Beige script paper (638983)
- Black and checkered ribbons
- Black cardstock (631007)
- Black script paper (660663)
- Black-with-beige-dots paper (660670)
- Book text
- Brown inkpad
- Brown watercolor pencil
- Cotton ball or manicure pad
- Cotton swab
- Craft glue
- Craft scissors
- "Halloween" sticker
- Jump rings
- Masking tape
- Matte gel medium
- Orange felt trim
- Pumpkin embossed sticker (551367)
- Ruler
- Tape runner adhesive

Directions

1. Cut two 3¾" x 8½" pieces of black cardstock for the cover and back of the card. Cut the beige script paper to 3¾" x 8½". Punch 1" circles from the black-with-beige-dots paper.

2. Using matte gel medium, adhere the circles to the beige script paper, then adhere the paper to a black cardstock piece. Create shadows for the circles by drawing around each one with a brown watercolor pencil then dragging a damp cotton swab over the marks. Use strips of masking tape to peel the top layer from the script paper (see "Peeling Paper," page 17). Age the card using brown ink and a cotton ball or manicure pad (see "Aging Paper," page 16).

3. Trim 1½" from the top of the paper-covered cardstock piece and use tape runner adhesive to adhere this 1½" strip to the top of the second cardstock piece. Place the remainder of the paper-covered black cardstock piece over the second cardstock piece, aligning its top edge with the bottom edge of the 1½" strip. While holding this in place, punch three ⅛" holes above the cut line, then punch three corresponding holes below the cut line. Place a jump ring through each set of holes (see "Attaching Jump Rings," page 16). Tie black and checkered ribbons to the jump rings. *Note: The card will open at these jump ring "hinges."*

4. Cut the black script paper to 3¾" x 3" and adhere it to the card. Apply the pumpkin embossed sticker to a piece of black cardstock and cut out the pumpkin. Attach the pumpkin to the card with foam tape. Use craft glue to adhere the orange felt trim, the "Halloween" sticker, and book text for "Boo" to the card.

Trick or Treat

Witches' Night Out Card

This invitation is so bewitching, your Halloween party guests will want to keep it as a souvenir.

Materials

— Black cardstock (631007)
— Black label-style alphabet stickers (667099)
— Black netting
— Black-with-beige-dots paper (660670)
— Craft scissors
— Ivory cardstock (630918)
— Lime-green textured paper (638938)
— Marker
— Prong fastener
— Ruler
— Stylus
— Tape runner adhesive
— Witch dimensional sticker (555846)

Directions

1. Cut black cardstock to 10" x 5". Create a tri-fold card by scoring vertically 2" from the left edge of the cardstock and again at 6" from the left edge. Fold in the right panel then fold in the left.

2. Cut the black-with-beige-dots paper into two 4" x 5" pieces. Adhere to the front and back of the right panel using tape runner adhesive. Cut the lime-green textured paper to two 2" x 4¹/2" pieces. Adhere to the front and back of the left panel.

3. Cut a 3" square from black cardstock. Use tape runner adhesive to adhere the square to the inside of the left panel at the center of the card. Fold in the left panel then apply the witch dimensional sticker to the center of the left panel and black square. Apply the black label-style alphabet stickers for "Witches' Night Out" around the moon of the dimensional sticker. *Note: If your witch sticker does not have a moon, you can create one by adding glitter to an ivory cardstock circle and adhering it to the card with foam tape before applying the witch image.*

4. Use a marker to handwrite the party details onto a 3¹/2" x 4¹/2" piece of ivory cardstock. *Note: You can use a computer and printer to create the text instead.* Cut a jagged edge along the bottom. Attach the cardstock and black netting to the inside of the card with a prong fastener.

WITCHES' NIGHT OUT

Welcome Ghouls Party Card

Combining a vintage clown with a jack-o'-lantern creates a cute Halloween character for this party invitation. Change the colors and it becomes a clown for a birthday card.

Materials

— 3⅜" circle template
— Beige-with-black-dots paper (661288)
— Beige script paper (638983)
— Black cardstock (631007)
— Black crepe-paper streamers
— Black label-style alphabet stickers (667099)
— Black text paper (660663)
— Black-with-beige-dots paper (660670)
— Craft glue
— Craft scissors
— Needle and black thread
— Peach-colored paper (660731)
— Pinking shears
— Round brass frames (558281)
— Ruler
— Tape runner adhesive

Directions

1. Cut the black cardstock to 7½" x 8½". Score and fold it in half to make a 3¾" x 8½" card. Cut the black text paper to 3¾" x 8½". Adhere the paper to the cover using tape runner adhesive. Cut the beige-with-black-dots paper to 3¾" x 4" and adhere to the bottom of the cover.

2. Trace the circle template onto peach-colored paper. Cut out and adhere this "head" to the cover using tape runner adhesive. Cut out eyes, a nose, and a mouth from the black-with-beige-dots paper and adhere to the head.

3. Cut a triangle from the beige script paper for a hat. Trim the sides of the hat with pinking shears. Cut long, narrow strips from black crepe-paper streamers. Using tape runner adhesive, adhere the streamers to the back of the hat at the top, then adhere the completed hat to the card.

4. Cut three 12" strips from the black crepe streamers. Stack the strips on top of each other and sew a running stitch through the center lengthwise. Carefully pull the thread to gather the streamers to the length of the collar. Secure the ends of the thread by making several small stitches and knotting the ends. Fold the stack in half lengthwise and adhere it to the card using craft glue.

5. Use black label-style alphabet stickers to spell "Welcome Ghouls" at the bottom of the cover. Use craft glue to adhere two round frames to the card for buttons.

Trick or Treat

Vintage Holidays

she
admired
his
holiday
spirit
25

The tradition of holiday greeting cards is important because it allows us to connect with the family and friends we don't often see. The holidays, with their age-old traditions and familiar motifs, are a perfect fit for vintage. The elegant, rich textures and colors of holiday seasons lend themselves beautifully to artfully crafted cards.

Thanksgiving Card

The earthy colors and vintage look of an embossed Thanksgiving sticker inspired this holiday card. The dimension of the sticker I chose allowed me to distress it easily by lightly rubbing over the top with fine sandpaper.

Materials

— Book dart (metal book marker)
— Brown textured paper (660694)
— Chipboard
— Computer and printer
— Craft scissors
— Embossed turkey sticker (551107)
— Gingham paper (638822)
— Ivory cardstock (630918)
— Large alphabet stickers (553590)
— Ruler
— Sewing machine and thread
— Stapler and staples
— Tape runner adhesive

Directions

1. Cut ivory cardstock to 10" x 7". Score and fold in half to make a 5" x 7" card. Cut the gingham paper to 5" x 7", then adhere to the cover using tape runner adhesive. Cut brown textured paper to 5" x 7". Tear off the right side of the paper and adhere it vertically to the cover.

2. Apply the large alphabet stickers for "Bless" to the cover. Using a computer, type and print out the words "Joy Thrives in the Soul of Thanksgiving" onto ivory cardstock and adhere it to the cover. Staple the book dart to the cover.

3. Apply an embossed turkey sticker to chipboard. Sew to the card with zigzag stitching.

Christmas Joy Card

The empty border left behind after an alphabet sticker has been pulled from its sheet can make appealing text. This design uses such "alphabet negatives" and a round frame to create an unusual title.

Materials

— ¼"-wide ribbons in brown and gingham
— Brown textured paper (660694)
— Brown with green dots paper (660687)
— Craft glue
— Craft scissors
— Ivory cardstock (630918)
— Large stencil-style alphabet stickers (553699)
— Narrow tan rickrack
— Round frame (564701)
— Ruler
— Small jingle bell
— Small page clip (564664)
— Tape runner adhesive
— "To" and "You" word brads (564671)

Directions

1. Cut ivory cardstock to 7" x 10". Score and fold it in half to make a 7" x 5" card.

2. Cut the brown-with-green-dots paper to 7" x 5". Use tape runner adhesive to adhere it to the cover. Cut the brown textured paper to 6" x 5" and adhere it to the cover, centering it so that ½" of the brown-with-green-dots paper remains visible on either side. Use craft glue to adhere narrow tan rickrack along the paper seams.

3. Attach the ribbons and jingle bell to a small page clip. Peel the J negative from the large stencil-style alphabet stickers and attach the page clip to it. Apply the J negative to the card. Peel the Y negative from the alphabet stickers, then add the "To" and "You" brads to it. Apply the Y negative to the card.

4. Using a computer, type and print out the word "Christmas" onto ivory cardstock, then cut it out in a strip. Use craft glue to adhere the round frame and the cardstock strip to the cover.

Vintage Holidays

Pure Joy Gift Card Enclosure

This card can be used to hold items other than just gift cards. You can enclose a family photo with a hand-written summary of your happenings over the past year or a phone card to entice a distant friend to get in touch.

Materials

— 1" circle punch
— Bell charm (558762)
— Brown colored pencil
— Craft scissors
— Glassine envelope
— Green patterned paper (660892)
— Ivory cardstock (630918)
— Jump ring
— Patchwork-style paper (660816)
— Pencil
— Pocket pattern (page 142)
— "Pure Joy" dimensional sticker (555952)
— Silver tinsel stems
— "Special" file tab (550377)
— Striped paper (660762)
— Tape runner adhesive

Directions

1. Trace the pocket pattern onto ivory cardstock and cut out. Fold in the right panel of the tag. Apply tape runner adhesive along the edge of the left panel, then fold it in and adhere it to the right panel. Apply tape runner adhesive to the bottom panel, then fold it in and adhere.

2. Cut the green patterned paper to the size of the pocket front. Use tape runner adhesive to adhere the paper to the pocket front.

3. Punch 1" circles from the patchwork-style paper. Use tape runner adhesive to adhere the circles to the pocket front, allowing some to extend past the edges. Trim off the extending circles. Draw a line around each circle with the brown colored pencil.

4. Wrap the silver tinsel stems around the pocket and twist together at the front of the pocket. Loosely coil the ends of the stems. Place a jump ring onto a bell charm and attach it to the tinsel stem. Apply the "Pure Joy" dimensional sticker to the pocket.

5. Cut ivory cardstock to 3" x 7" to make the card insert. Cut the striped paper to 3" x 7" and adhere to the card using tape runner adhesive. Adhere the glassine envelope to the card. Cut the green patterned paper to 3" x 2½" and adhere to the glassine envelope. Adhere the "Special" file tab to the top of the card. Slide the card into the pocket.

Vintage Holidays

Peace Card

A gold leafing pen adds a luxurious, classic touch to holiday cards. As an alternative, apply gold acrylic paint around the card edges.

Materials

— Alphabet stickers (553316)
— Craft scissors
— Gold floral paper (637900)
— Gold leafing pen
— Large oval frame sticker (551824)
— Metallic gold embroidery floss
— Metallic gold rickrack
— Plain card (240155)
— Red patterned paper (639041)
— Ruler
— Small border stickers (553316)
— Stapler and staples
— Tape runner adhesive

Directions

1. Cut the red patterned paper to the size of the cover of the plain card. Adhere the paper to the cover using tape runner adhesive.

2. Cut a 5½" x 1" strip of gold floral paper and adhere horizontally to the center of the cover using tape runner adhesive. Apply small border stickers to the top and bottom edges of the gold floral strip.

3. Apply a large oval frame sticker to the cover. Peel the letter P from the alphabet stickers and tie a few strands of metallic gold embroidery floss to it. Apply the sticker to the cover then apply the remaining letters to spell "Peace."

4. Fold and staple metallic gold rickrack to the cover. Accent the edges of the card with the gold leafing pen.

she

admired

his

holiday

spirit

Holiday Spirit Tag

This tag not only adds appeal to a gift, but its fun details and small size mean it can be displayed as an ornament on the tree.

Materials

— ⅛" hole punch
— 1½" circle punch
— Alphabet stamps (Inkadinkado 94146)
— Ball chain
— Black gingham paper (661240)
— Brown inkpad
— Computer and printer
— Craft glue
— Craft scissors
— Foam tape
— Green stitched ribbon (543034)
— Green textured paper (660380)
— Ivory cardstock (630918)
— Number stickers (553316)
— O letter tile (563544)
— Postcard-themed paper (661219)
— Red fringed yarn
— Red paper (635104)
— Red stitched ribbon (543027)
— Shipping tag
— Tape runner adhesive
— Vintage sports figure cut-out (638679)

Directions

1. Cut the postcard-themed paper to the size and shape of the shipping tag. Adhere the paper to the tag using tape runner adhesive. Cut a 1"-wide strip of black gingham paper the length of the tag's width and adhere it to the bottom of the tag.

2. Punch a 1½" circle from green textured paper and adhere to the tag. Using a computer, type and print the words "she admired his holiday spirit" onto a strip of ivory cardstock. Cut out each word and adhere down the side of the tag.

3. Tie a length of red fringed yarn around the vintage sports figure's neck for a scarf. Cut a tall triangle "hat" from the red paper. Adhere the figure and hat to the tag using tape runner adhesive. Cut a small strip from the postcard-themed paper for the figure's hat brim and adhere it to the hat using foam tape.

4. Stamp "Ho Ho Ho" across the top with brown ink. Use craft glue to adhere the O letter tile to the point of the hat and over the O of the second "Ho."

5. Apply the number 2 and 5 stickers to the tag. Using craft glue, adhere the green and red stitched ribbons to the back of the tag.

6. Punch a hole at the top of the tag and attach the ball chain.

Vintage Holidays

Believe Card

Add texture to Santa's beard and coat trim with gel medium, molding paste, or caulking. Paint or stain the added texture to maintain the vintage look of the card.

Materials
— "Believe" sticker (551268)
— Brass border (558632)
— Brown acrylic paint
— Brown inkpad
— Chipboard
— Cotton ball or manicure pad
— Craft knife
— Craft scissors
— Fine sandpaper
— Gold floral paper (637900)
— Gold holly leaves
— Ivory cardstock (630918)
— Mini brads
— Paintbrush
— Postcard-themed paper (661219)
— Red binder clip
— Red diamond paper (633674)
— Ribbon (257016)
— Ruler
— Stapler and staples
— Tape runner adhesive
— Vintage Santa image (551817)

Directions

1. Cut the chipboard to 3$\frac{1}{2}$" x 6". Cut the gold floral paper to 3$\frac{1}{2}$" x 6" and adhere it to the chipboard using tape runner adhesive.

2. Cut ivory cardstock and red diamond paper to 3$\frac{1}{2}$" x 6" and adhere the two papers together using tape runner adhesive. Using a craft knife, cut a 2$\frac{1}{4}$" x 5" "door" from the center, leaving its top edge uncut to act as a hinge. To make sure the recipient can open the door easily, cut a half circle from the outside bottom edge of the doorframe. Adhere the entire card-stock piece to the covered chipboard piece along the outside edges of the doorframe.

3. Cut the gold floral paper to be slightly smaller than the door of the card and adhere it to the front of the door, then adhere the vintage Santa image to the gold floral paper. Distress the image by rubbing fine sandpaper over the top of the sticker then age it using brown ink and a cotton ball or manicure pad (see "Aging Paper," page 16). Cut a square from the postcard-themed paper, wrap it around the edge of the door and adhere. Apply the "Believe" sticker to the Santa image.

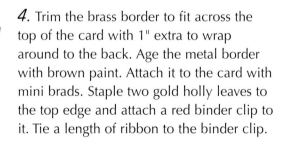

4. Trim the brass border to fit across the top of the card with 1" extra to wrap around to the back. Age the metal border with brown paint. Attach it to the card with mini brads. Staple two gold holly leaves to the top edge and attach a red binder clip to it. Tie a length of ribbon to the binder clip.

Vintage Holidays

merry CHRISTMAS

oh so nice

Naughty nice

Naughty... naughty naughty!

as nice as can be

to a sweet TEACHER

Sno·ette

Retro Christmas

For the holidays, the retro look is just plain fun. The bold geometrics, graphic designs, and bright colors have an energy that makes retro a cheerful alternative to vintage while still evoking memories from yesteryear. Turn on some Christmas oldies and enjoy yourself while making these cards.

Merry Christmas Card

The snowflakes on this card are simple motifs cut from patterned paper. Add silver squares to the tops of these circles and they become ornaments.

Materials

— Craft scissors
— Glittery snowflakes paper (641457)
— Ivory cardstock (630918)
— Lime-green dotted paper (660700)
— "Merry Christmas" transfer (590236)
— Red checked paper (436213)
— Red stitches transfer (590144)
— Ruler
— Tape runner adhesive

Directions

1. Cut ivory cardstock to 7¹/₂" x 8¹/₂". Score and fold it in half to make a 3³/₄" x 8¹/₂" card. Trim ³/₄" from the right side of the cover.

2. Cut the lime-green dotted paper to 3" x 8¹/₂" and adhere it to the cover using tape runner adhesive. Apply the red stitches transfer along the right edge of the cover. Cut circles around three snowflakes from the glittery snowflakes paper. Adhere the circles to the card. Apply the "Merry Christmas" transfer between the circles.

3. Cut the red checked paper to 3³/₄" x 8¹/₂". Adhere to the inside of the card using tape runner adhesive.

Let It Snow Tag

Creating a tag from acetate is a nice change from paper since the items you place inside, such as photos or embellishments, can be an integral part of the design.

Materials

— Craft scissors

— Gel superglue

— Red metallic cord

— Red tulle

— Red yarn

— Ruler

— Script acetate (661004)

— Sewing machine and white thread

— Silver miniature tree garland

— Silver rectangular label frame (563230)

— Snowflake sequins

— Stapler and staples

— Tiny glass marbles

— Velvet ribbon

Directions

1. Cut the script acetate to 3" x 8" and fold it in half, matching the short edges. Use gel superglue to adhere snowflake sequins to the inside. Sew around the acetate tag along three edges to form a pocket. Place tiny glass marbles in the pocket and enclose by sewing the remaining edge.

2. Staple velvet ribbon across the front of the tag. Tie tulle, yarn, and miniature tree garland to the silver rectangular label frame. Add a length of red metallic cord to the tag for a hanger. Use gel superglue to attach this completed piece to the top of the acetate tag.

Retro Christmas

Naughty or Nice? Card

My son inspired this card. I'm always reminding him that Santa is watching! To customize the design, write your own spinner choice in each section.

Materials

- 1¼" circle punch
- 4½" circle template
- Adhesive foam dots
- Black acrylic paint
- Black cardstock (631007)
- Black elastic
- Black inkpad
- Black marker
- Brad
- Craft glue
- Craft scissors
- "Dare to Be Yourself" stamp (Inkadinkado 94893)
- Lime-green dotted paper (660700)
- Metal game spinner
- Paintbrush
- Red checked fabric
- Red dotted paper (436152)
- Red swirls paper (436107)
- Ruler
- Small round frames (558250)
- Stapler and staples
- Tape runner adhesive
- White cardstock (630901)

Directions

1. Cut black cardstock to 6" x 12". Score and fold it in half to make a 6" x 6" card with the fold at the top.

2. Cut the red swirls paper to be slightly smaller than the cover and use tape runner adhesive to adhere it to the cover. Trace the 4½" circle template onto lime-green dotted paper.

3. Cut out the circle then cut it into six equal wedges and adhere them to the card, leaving spaces between the wedges. Handwrite a different spinner choice onto each wedge.

4. Punch a 1¼" circle from the red dotted paper and black cardstock. Adhere the two circles together using tape runner adhesive. Adhere foam dots to the back of the circle. Paint the metal game spinner black. Use a brad to attach the spinner to the circle and then to the card.

5. Stamp "Dare to Be Yourself" in black ink onto a strip of white cardstock. Staple the strip to the card. Use craft glue to adhere three round frames to the card.

6. Tie a length of black elastic around the card at the fold. Tie strips of red check fabric to the elastic.

so **nice**

Naughty

Naughty... naughty... naughty!

as **Nice** can be

Shame on You!

Nice

Dare To Be Yourself

Sweet Teacher Card

This sweet sentiment lets a special teacher know she is appreciated. Send it to school along with a plate of treats in pretty wrapping.

Materials

— Black marker
— Cellophane
— Candy-cane-striped paper (639362)
— Computer and printer
— Craft scissors
— Ivory Cardstock (630918)
— Ribbon (257016)
— Ruler
— Tape runner adhesive
— White cardstock (630901)

Directions

1. Cut the ivory cardstock to 6" x 7". Fold in half to make a 6" x 3½" card. Cut the candy-cane-striped paper to 6" x 3½" and adhere it to the cover using tape runner adhesive.

2. Using a computer, type and print the word "Teacher" onto white cardstock. Cut out the letters in blocks and adhere them to the card. Handwrite "To a sweet" above the word "Teacher."

3. Cut the cellophane to approximately 18" x 8". Fold and center the cellophane to stretch across inside of card and adhere it in place using tape runner adhesive. Tie lengths of ribbon around cellophane at each end and tighten them to gather the cellophane. Trim the cellophane if needed.

4. Cut the candy-cane-striped paper to 6" x 3½" and adhere it to the inside of the card, covering the inside edges of the cellophane.

to a sweet

TEACHER

Retro Christmas

Winter Wish Card

A shimmering tinsel wand with "magic" made of white sparkly yarn promises to grant the recipient a seasonal wish.

Materials

— 1" circle punch
— 1^1/$_2$" circle punch
— 1^1/$_4$" circle punch
— Black cardstock (631007)
— Computer and printer
— Craft glue
— Craft scissors
— Foam tape
— Lime-green paper (638938)
— Pinking shears
— Red dotted paper (436152)
— Red swirls paper (436107)
— Ruler
— Script acetate (660991)
— Silver mini brads
— Silver tinsel stems
— Tape runner adhesive
— White sparkly yarn

Directions

1. Cut the black cardstock to 7^1/$_2$" x 8^1/$_2$". Score and fold it in half to make a 3^3/$_4$" x 8^1/$_2$" card. Cut the red dotted paper and script acetate to 3^3/$_4$" x 8^1/$_2$". Lay the acetate over the paper and attach them together at the corners with four silver mini brads. Adhere this completed piece to the card cover using tape runner adhesive.

2. Coil the end of one silver tinsel stem into a small circle. Form a looped handle at the other end of this "wand."

3. Punch two 1^1/$_2$" circles from the lime-green paper and two 1^1/$_4$" circles from the red swirls paper. Adhere the 1^1/$_2$" circles on the underside of the wand stem using craft glue. Adhere the 1^1/$_4$" circles on top of the wand stem, centering each one over each 1^1/$_2$" circle. Attach the smaller circles to the larger circles with foam tape on each side of the wand stem. Assemble the crossbar of the wand in the same manner with two 1" and 1^1/$_4$" circles and a 5^1/$_2$" length of silver tinsel stem. Coil the ends of this stem. Tie lengths of white sparkly yarn to the wand. Use craft glue to attach the wand to the card.

4. Using a computer, type and print the words "A Winter Wish" onto the lime-green paper. Trim around the title with pinking shears. Adhere to the card using tape runner adhesive.

Sweet Nothings

Romantic cards can be cherished tokens of affection. Handmade cards make your sentiments even more meaningful, so bypass the store-bought cards on Valentine's Day, and take time to add something more to your next anniversary celebration. Better yet, use one of the following designs to surprise your sweetie for no reason at all.

Guilty of Loving You Card

The soundtrack of a French film inspired me to create this card. It's so melodramatic, the person who receives it will just have to smile.

Materials

— Black cardstock (631007)
— Black label-style alphabet stickers (667099)
— Black text paper (660663)
— Black wire
— Brown-with-green-dots paper (660687)
— Craft knife
— Craft scissors
— Embossed alphabet stickers (667082)
— Eyelet setter and black eyelets
— Green textured paper (660892)
— Lock charm (558373)
— Needle-nosed pliers
— Ruler
— Tape runner adhesive

Directions

1. Cut black cardstock to 7$\frac{1}{2}$" x 9". Score and fold it in half to make a 3$\frac{3}{4}$" x 9" card.

2. Cut the black text paper to 3$\frac{3}{4}$" x 9" and adhere it to the cover of the card using tape runner adhesive.

3. Use a craft knife to cut a 2$\frac{1}{4}$" x 3$\frac{1}{2}$" window from the top portion of the cover (see "Cutting Out Windows," page 17). Set three eyelets on either side of the window. Set two eyelets above and two below the window.

4. Cut three lengths of black wire to stretch horizontally and two lengths to stretch vertically across the window. Thread the ends of four lengths of wire through the eyelets and "knot" each end by coiling the wire with needle-nosed pliers. Wind the fifth length of wire around a lock charm, then attach the wire to the remaining set of eyelets as indicated above.

5. Apply the embossed alphabet stickers to the card to spell "Guilty." Cut a 4" x $\frac{3}{4}$" strip from the green textured paper. Adhere across the cover. Trim the edges as necessary. Apply black label-style alphabet stickers to the strip to spell "Of Loving You."

6. Cut a heart from the brown-with-green-dots paper and use tape runner adhesive to adhere it to the inside of the card, placing it so that the heart appears in the window when the card is closed.

Sweet Nothings

How Do I Love Thee Card

A phrase from a Shakespearean sonnet lends itself perfectly to a romantic card. Numbered petals enhance this design's "counting" theme.

Materials

— $\frac{1}{8}$" hole punch
— $2\frac{1}{4}$" circle template
— Brad
— Brown-with-green-dots paper (660687)
— Chipboard
— Craft scissors
— Five different sentiments stickers (667068)
— Green patterned paper (661028)
— Green textured paper (660892)
— Green-with-brown-circles paper (660823)
— "How Do I Love Thee" dimensional sticker (555952)
— Ivory cardstock (630918)
— Numbers paper (660717)
— Pencil
— Petal pattern (page 140)
— Ribbons
— Tape runner adhesive
— Text-with-dots paper (660786)

Directions

1. Trace the petal pattern five times onto ivory cardstock and once onto each of the five decorative papers. Cut out the petals. Adhere the cardstock petals to each paper petal using tape runner adhesive.

2. Cut out the numbers 1 through 5 from the numbers paper in rectangles and adhere one to each petal using tape runner adhesive. Apply a different sentiment sticker to each petal. *Note: If you can't find the sentiment stickers you want, use a computer to type and print text onto cardstock and adhere to the petals with tape runner adhesive.*

3. Using the $2\frac{1}{4}$" circle template, trace two circles onto chip board and cut them out. Punch five holes along the bottom edge of one chipboard circle. Tie ribbons to each hole.

4. Stack and align the petals with the number 1 on top and the rest in order. Place the bottom end of the stack on the ribbon-embellished chipboard circle. Place the second chipboard circle on top of the stack. Place a brad through the center of all the layers.

5. Cut the brown-with-green-dots paper to the size of the top circle and adhere it to the circle. Apply the "How Do I Love Thee" dimensional sticker to the top circle.

Love You Card

In this design, rub-on transfers give the illusion of stitching along the paper "seams" between the letters. Cut each transfer stitch apart before applying it to the card to save yourself from applying unwanted stitches.

Materials

— Craft glue

— Craft knife

— Craft scissors

— Domed black alphabet stickers (665163)

— Fiber

— Green textured paper (660892)

— Ivory cardstock (630918)

— Large stencil-style alphabet stickers (553699)

— Plastic microscope slide

— Polka-dots-on-text paper (660786)

— Ribbons of various widths in green and brown

— Round copper frame (563438)

— Ruler

— Stitch transfers (590151)

— Tape runner adhesive

Directions

1. Cut ivory cardstock to 9$^{1}/_{2}$" x 6$^{1}/_{2}$". Score and fold it in half to make a 4$^{3}/_{4}$" x 6$^{1}/_{2}$" card. Cut the polka-dots-on-text paper to 4$^{3}/_{4}$" x 6$^{1}/_{2}$" and adhere it to the cover using tape runner adhesive.

2. Apply the large stencil-style alphabet stickers L, V, and E to the card. Apply the stitch transfers along the edges of the alphabet stickers (see "Applying Rub-on Transfers," page 16).

3. Use a craft knife to cut a window in the cover, using the interior of the round copper frame as a template (see "Cutting Out Windows," page 17). Trim and adhere the plastic microscope slide across the window using craft glue. Tie ribbons and fiber to the frame and adhere it to the card to become the O in "Love." Apply the domed black alphabet stickers for "You" to the slide.

4. Cut the green textured paper to 4$^{3}/_{4}$" x 6$^{1}/_{2}$". Adhere to the inside of the card using tape runner adhesive.

Sweet Nothings

Forever 2 Card

The red paper used for this anniversary card has a plain white back. Ink rubbed across its embossed surface and a layer of acetate add dimension to the design.

Materials
- Ball chain
- Black cardstock (631007)
- Black gingham paper (661240)
- Black marker
- Black stitched ribbon (543003)
- Black-with-cream-pattern paper (661257)
- Brown inkpad
- Clock image brad (564763)
- Cotton ball or manicure pad
- Craft glue and scissors
- Cream-and-text paper (661202)
- Eyelet setter and a black eyelet
- "Forever" transfer (590380)
- Heart charm (564176)
- "He Loves Me" sticker (667068)
- Ivory cardstock (630918)
- Ivory-with-brown-dots paper (661288)
- Patterned acetate (661387)
- Large number stickers (553408)
- Large photo clasps (563810)
- Pinking shears
- Red floral embossed paper (641747)
- Ruler
- Sandpaper
- Small photo clasps (563810)
- Stapler and staples
- Tape runner adhesive

Directions

1. To create the bottom layer of the card, cut the black cardstock to 5¼" x 5". Trim the right side with pinking shears.

2. To create the middle layer of the card, cut the red floral embossed paper to 5" x 5". Turn the paper over and rub brown ink over the plain white side with a cotton ball or manicure pad. Use craft glue to adhere pieces of black-with-cream-pattern, cream-and-text, black gingham, and ivory-with-brown-dots papers to the top of four large photo clasps. Trim the paper around the photo clasps by rubbing sandpaper across the metal edges of the clasps. Apply craft glue to these "flower petals" and stack them on top of each other, aligning the holes. Place the clock image brad through the holes and secure at the back. Cover a small photo clasp in the same manner with black-with-cream-pattern paper.

3. To create the top layer of the card, cut the patterned acetate to 5" x 5". Cut two 2½" squares from the red floral embossed paper. Adhere the photo clasp "flower" to the red side of one of the squares. Adhere the single petal and apply the "He Loves Me" sticker to the same square. Use tape runner adhesive to adhere the square to the lower right corner of the acetate piece and the remaining 2½" square to the opposite corner, red side out. Apply the large number sticker 2 to the upper left floral embossed square. Apply the "Forever" transfer over the 2.

4. Group the layers together and set an eyelet through them at the top left corner. Thread the ball chain through the eyelet. Tie a heart charm to the ball chain with ribbon. Cut a small tag from ivory cardstock then tie it with a black stitched ribbon to the ball chain. Use the black marker to write "Happy Anniversary" on it. Staple lengths of stitched ribbon between the acetate and reversed embossed paper layers.

forever 2

IAGE -jnos

he loves me

Fills My Heart Card

When this card's tag is pulled up, red paper appears underneath, making the heart look as though it is being filled from the bottom up.

Materials

— Black-and-dotted paper (661233)
— Black elastic cord
— Black label-style alphabet stickers (667099)
— Black marker
— "Cherish" file tab (550360)
— Craft knife
— Craft scissors
— Heart pattern (page 139)
— Ivory cardstock (630918)
— Pencil
— Red cardstock (631045)
— Ruler
— Scalloped scissors
— Script acetate (660991)
— Sewing machine and beige thread
— Stapler and staples
— Tape runner adhesive

Directions

1. Cut ivory cardstock to $3\frac{1}{2}$" x 12". Score and fold it in half to make a $3\frac{1}{2}$" x 6" card.

2. Cut the black-and-dotted paper to the size of the card. Adhere it to the cover using tape runner adhesive. Cut out a half-circle notch at the top of the card. Trace the heart pattern onto the cover and use a craft knife to cut a heart-shaped window (see "Cutting Out Windows," page 17). Adhere a piece of script acetate behind the window.

3. Cut the red cardstock to $4\frac{1}{2}$" x 6" and trim the left and right sides with scalloped scissors. Place the red cardstock piece between the card layers. Sew the card together at the left and right edges to create a sleeve.

4. Apply black label-style alphabet stickers to ivory cardstock to create the sentiment "Your Love Fills My Heart." Cut out the words and adhere them to the card.

5. Cut a tag from ivory cardstock. *Note: The tag should fit inside the sleeve and extend just past the bottom tip of the heart window.* Round off the corners of the tag. Adhere the "Cherish" file tab to the top of the tag.

6. Cut a small strip from red cardstock. Fold the cardstock strip in half and wrap it around the black elastic cord to create a tab. Adhere the ends of the strip together using tape runner adhesive. Use the black marker to write "Pull" on the tab. Loop the black elastic cord, knot the ends, and staple the card to the file tab.

Pull

Cherish

YOUR LOVE FILLS MY HEART

Sweet Nothings

Love Always Card

Looking for multiple ways to use materials can lead to rewarding discoveries. For this card, the circle clasp serves as a hanger for a heart charm.

Materials

— "Always" transfer (590120)
— Circle string clasp (542631)
— Craft scissors
— Embossed Cupid sticker (551107)
— Faded red paper (ACS-045)
— Heart charm (564176)
— Heart foam stamp
— Jump ring
— Large alphabet stickers (553415)
— Red fiber
— Red ink
— Ruler
— Tape runner adhesive
— Vintage floral paper (ACS-050)

Directions

1. Cut the faded red paper to 10" x 7". Score and fold it in half to make a 5" x 7" card. Cut the vintage floral paper to 5" x 3³/₄" and adhere it to the center of the card using tape runner adhesive.

2. Stamp the heart image onto the card using red ink. Apply the embossed Cupid sticker and the large alphabet stickers to spell "Love."

3. Apply a circle string clasp to the card. Attach a jump ring to the heart charm. Thread a length of red fiber through the jump ring and tie it at the center. Wrap the fiber ends around the circle clasp and tie a knot.

4. Apply the "Always" transfer to the card.

Sweet Nothings

THANKS FOR LISTENING

THANKS friend

The truth is she just loves laughing

MERCI

is where you find it.

Saying Thank You

I can't think of a better way to reciprocate someone's generosity, kindness, and selflessness than with a handmade thank-you card. Giving the gift of your time and thoughtfulness shows your true appreciation and allows you to connect on a deeper level with family, friends, and neighbors.

Merci Card

This card features a simple background so that the intricate flower remains the focus. A pin back is attached to the flower so that it can be worn.

Materials

— Black label-style alphabet stickers (667099)
— Black netting
— Black-with-cream-pattern paper (661257)
— Clear jewels
— Craft glue
— Craft scissors
— Crushed suede fabric
— Fabric scissors
— Gel superglue
— Ivory cardstock (630918)
— Large round brass frame (558304)
— Moiré fabric
— Needle and thread
— Pin back
— Ruler
— Stitched border (542006)
— Tape runner adhesive
— Text strips paper (661202)

Directions

1. Cut ivory cardstock to 10" x 7". Score and fold it in half to make a 5" x 7" card.

2. Cut the black-with-cream-pattern paper to 5" x 7" and adhere it to the cover using tape runner adhesive. Cut the text strips paper to 5" x 3" and adhere it to the bottom of the card. Place the stitched border across the top of the text strips paper and trim it to fit.

3. *Note: The flower pin is created with three layers of fabric.* Cut a 2"-wide strip of crushed suede fabric to 9". Scallop the top of the strip to form six flower petals. Sew a running stitch 1/4" from the base of the strip and pull the thread to gather the fabric. Form the gathered fabric into a circle and stitch the ends together. *Note: This is the bottom layer of the flower pin.* Repeat this process with black netting to complete the second layer of the flower. Repeat this process with a 1 1/2" x 6" strip of moiré fabric to complete the top layer of the flower. Sew the three layers together at the center of the flower until secure.

4. Use craft glue to adhere a large round brass frame to the center of the flower. Use gel superglue to adhere clear jewels to the center. Stitch the pin back to the flower. Pin the flower to the card at the stitched border.

5. Apply the black label-style alphabet stickers to spell "Merci."

MERCI

Saying Thank You

Thanks for Listening Card

Look for different ways to use the shape of a premade card. The plain card used as the base of this project would normally be vertical, but here it is turned on its side. The flap is opened and its center is cut so that it resembles the handle of a coffee mug.

Materials

— "100% Friends" tag-shaped sticker (665170)
— Black inkpad
— Black label-style alphabet stickers (667099)
— Brown textured paper (660694)
— Corner rounder (optional)
— Craft glue
— Craft knife
— Craft scissors
— Cup stamp (Inkadinkado 92104 M)
— Embossed alphabet stickers (667082)
— Lime-green dotted paper (660700)
— Plain card with a flap (240162)
— Ribbon
— Ruler
— Scrap cardstock
— Tape runner adhesive
— Text-and-dots paper (660786)

Directions

1. Cut the brown textured paper to the size of the plain card's cover, excluding the flap. Adhere the paper to the cover using tape runner adhesive.

2. Open the card and adhere text-and-dots paper to the inside of the card, including the flap, using tape runner adhesive. Form a handle by rounding the top and bottom edges of the flap then use a craft knife to cut out the inside of the handle. Round off the corners of the card.

3. Apply embossed alphabet stickers to spell "Thanks" onto lime-green dotted paper. Cut out the letters in blocks and adhere them to the card using tape runner adhesive.

4. Cut a $5\frac{1}{4}"$ x 1" strip from the lime-green dotted paper. Cut this strip into three unequal pieces and adhere them to the card, leaving a space between each.

5. Stamp the cup image onto the card with black ink. Apply black label-style alphabet stickers to spell "For listening."

6. Apply the "100% Friends" tag-shaped sticker to a piece of scrap cardstock and cut it out. Adhere the mounted sticker to the cup handle using craft glue. Tie a length of ribbon to the handle above the cardstock tag and use craft glue to adhere the knot at the hole in the tag.

Thanks Friend Card

Because images printed on an inkjet printer will smear when wet, be sure to use a laser printer or color copier when printing or copying the photograph used for this design.

Materials

— 1/8" hole punch
— Amber bead
— Amber jewel
— Black label-style alphabet stickers (667099)
— Brass lace border (558618)
— Clear domed tags (557437)
— Color-copied photograph
— Craft scissors
— Eye pin
— Faux pearl beads
— "Friends" transfer (590380)
— Gel superglue

— Ivory cardstock (630918)
— Jump rings
— Peach diamonds paper (660731)
— Postcard-themed paper (661219)
— Round nose pliers
— Ruler
— Small script transfer (590373)
— Tape runner adhesive
— Wooden craft stick
— Word stickers for "The Truth is She Just Loves Laughing" (667068)

Directions

1. Cut ivory cardstock to 7 1/2" x 6". Score and fold it in half to make a 3 3/4" x 6" card.

2. Cut the postcard-themed paper to 3 3/4" x 6" and adhere it to the cover using tape runner adhesive. Cut peach diamonds paper to 2 1/2" x 6" and adhere it to the left side of the card.

3. Apply the small script transfer and the "Friends" transfer to the cover. Apply the black label-style alphabet stickers to the cover to spell "Thanks."

4. Apply a clear domed tag over the color-copied photograph. Cut around the edges of the tag. Turn over the tag and burnish the entire area with a wooden craft stick. Place the tag in water and let it soak for at least five minutes. Remove the tag from the water and carefully rub off the paper with your finger. Do this until all of the paper has been removed. Let it dry. Apply a second clear domed tag to the back of the image. Press the layered tags together tightly.

5. Cut a crown from a section of the brass lace border. Use gel superglue to adhere the amber jewel to the center of the crown. Adhere the crown to the layered tag.

6. Thread the amber and faux pearl beads onto the eye pin. Coil the opposite end with round nose pliers. Punch a hole at the bottom of the tag. Attach the bead dangle to the hole with a jump ring. Punch two small holes at the top of the card and attach the completed tag to the holes with a jump ring.

7. Apply word stickers to create the sentiment "The Truth is She Just Loves Laughing" to complete the card. *Note: If you can't find the right word stickers, use alphabet stickers instead.*

Grateful Tag

While experimenting with unusual ways to use my supplies, I discovered that by combining large photograph corners you can make a "pocket" for sentiments.

Materials

— 18-gauge wire
— Beads
— Black marker
— Brown acrylic paint
— Brown floral paper (661158)
— Chipboard
— Cotton swab
— Craft scissors
— Daisies paper (661103)
— Embossed floral stickers (551251)
— Flower-topped brads (564749)
— Foam tape
— Gesso
— "Happiness Is Where You Find It" sticker (551244)
— Ivory cardstock (630918)
— Light green acrylic paint
— Paintbrush
— Striped page corners (563834)
— Tag-shaped punch
— Tape runner adhesive

Directions

1. Cut chipboard to 4" x 6" and cut off the top corners to create a tag. Cut the brown floral paper to the size of the tag and adhere it to the tag using tape runner adhesive.

2. Paint two striped page corners with gesso. When dry, apply light green acrylic paint. Use the cotton swab to apply brown acrylic paint to the contours of the page corners. Let them dry completely. Adhere the corners together so that they will fit along the bottom portion of the tag, then attach them to the tag with strips of foam tape placed along the three straight edges to create a pocket.

3. Apply the "Happiness Is Where You Find It" sticker to the front of the pocket. *If you can't find a sticker with this sentiment on it, use alphabet stickers instead.* Apply an embossed floral sticker to ivory cardstock and cut out. Adhere to the pocket with foam tape.

4. Form a handle for the tag by threading beads onto a length of wire, making twists and coils as you go. Attach the ends of the handle to the tag with two flower-topped brads. Punch a tag from the daisies paper and use a wire end to attach it to the tag.

5. Handwrite various sentiments on strips of ivory cardstock and tuck them into the pocket.

Queen of the House Gift Card Enclosure

Several embellishments and layers of paper give this card a weight that makes it feel especially regal.

Materials

- 1" circle punch
- "All She Wanted was a Little Time" sentiment sticker (667068)
- Black alphabet stickers (553347)
- Black-with-beige-dots paper (660670)
- Computer and printer
- Craft glue
- Craft scissors
- Cream script paper (636361)
- Foam tape
- Foil paper border
- Gel superglue
- Ivory cardstock (630918)
- Key charm (558151
- Large scroll stamp
- Round silver frames (558298)
- Large alphabet stickers (553705)
- Paintbrush
- Pink acrylic paint
- Pink frame transfer (590069)
- Pink jewels
- Pink patterned paper (660748)
- Ruler
- Tape runner adhesive
- Tassel

Directions

1. Cut ivory cardstock to create a 10" x 7" rectangle. With the rectangle horizontal, score it vertically 2$\frac{1}{2}$" from the left edge. Repeat at 2$\frac{1}{2}$" from the right edge. Fold the sides to the center to create two front panels. Cut off the top corners to form house eaves.

2. Cut the black-with-beige-dots paper into two pieces the size of each front panel. Adhere the paper to the front panels using tape runner adhesive. Stamp a large scroll onto the cover with pink acrylic paint.

3. Apply the large alphabet sticker O to ivory cardstock. Cut it out. Apply the O to the card with foam tape. Tie the tassel to a key charm and, using foam tape, adhere the charm to the O to form the tail of the letter Q. Use gel superglue to adhere three pink jewels to the Q.

4. Apply a pink frame transfer to the lower right front panel of the card. Print or stamp the words "The Queen of the House" onto ivory cardstock and trim it to fit the frame. Apply the "All She Wanted was a Little Time" sentiment sticker to the right of the frame. *Note: If you can't find this sentiment on a sticker, you can stamp it on cardstock and adhere it in place.*

5. Cut the pink patterned paper into three pieces the size of the inside panels. Use tape runner adhesive to adhere each piece to the inside panels. Cut two 2$\frac{1}{2}$" x 2$\frac{1}{2}$" pieces and one 5" x 2$\frac{1}{2}$" piece of black-with-beige-dots paper. Adhere each piece to each panel bottom. Adhere the foil paper border along the top and bottom edges.

Instructions continued on page 138

gift
card

6. Apply black alphabet stickers to the cream script paper to spell "Royal." Cut out the letters in blocks and adhere to the inside of the card using tape runner adhesive. Using a computer, type and print the words "You Deserve The" and "Treatment" on ivory cardstock, cut them out, and adhere them to the inside of the card. Use gel superglue to adhere jewels below the word "Treatment."

7. Apply pink acrylic paint to both sides of three round frames. Punch five 1" circles from the cream script paper. Use craft glue to adhere a punched circle to the center of each frame and to adhere a frame to the inside of the card at the center peak of the crown. Close the card and adhere the remaining frames at the peaks of the front panels. Open the card and adhere a punched circle to the back of each outside frame.

Patterns

These patterns are at 100% of their intended size unless otherwise noted.
To use, trace or photocopy them onto plain paper and cut them out.

*Pattern for Fills My Heart
Card (p. 122)*

*Pattern for Birthday Bracelet
Card Page (p. 71)*

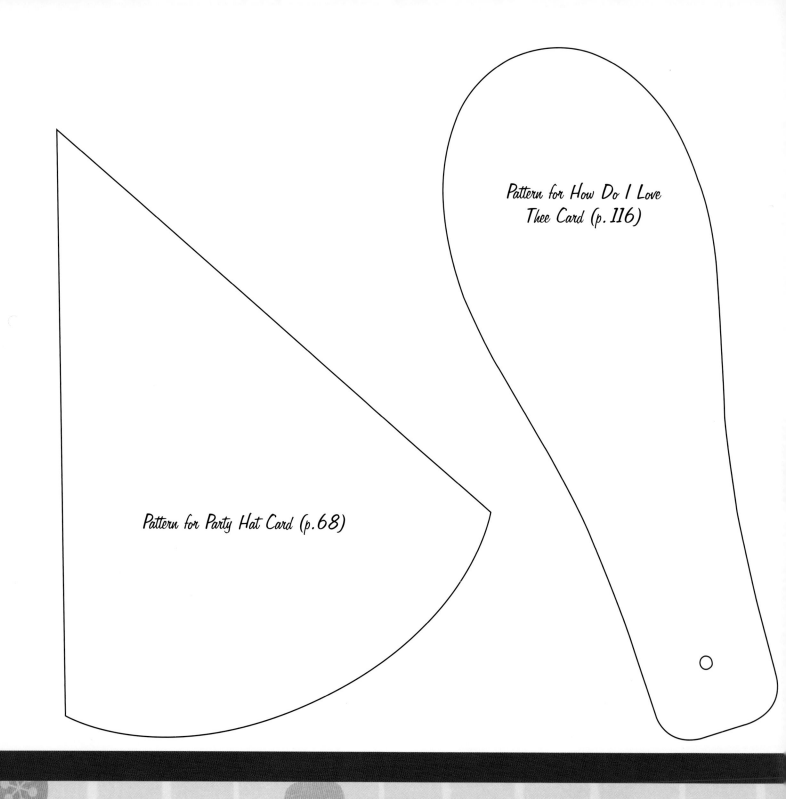

Pattern for How Do I Love
Thee Card (p. 116)

Pattern for Party Hat Card (p. 68)

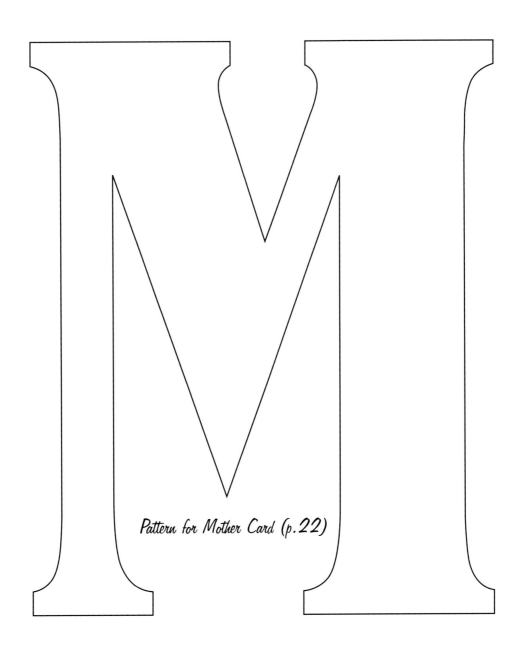

Pattern for Mother Card (p. 22)

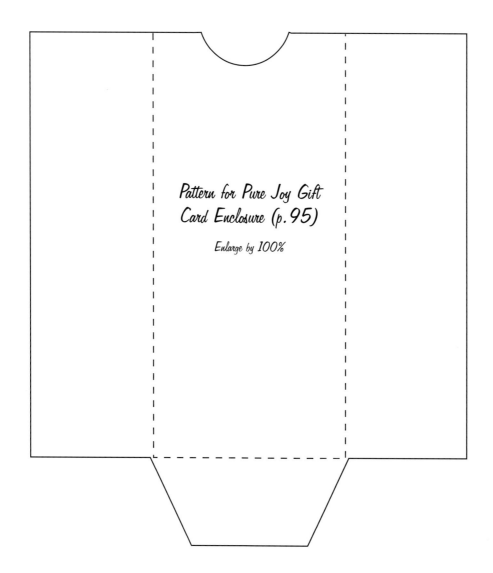

Pattern for Pure Joy Gift
Card Enclosure (p. 95)

Enlarge by 100%

Metric Conversion Chart

inches to millimeters and centimeters						
inches	mm	cm	inches	cm	inches	cm
⅛	3	0.3	9	22.9	30	76.2
¼	6	0.6	10	25.4	31	78.7
½	13	1.3	12	30.5	33	83.8
⅝	16	1.6	13	33.0	34	86.4
¾	19	1.9	14	35.6	35	88.9
⅞	22	2.2	15	38.1	36	91.4
1	25	2.5	16	40.6	37	94.0
1¼	32	3.2	17	43.2	38	96.5
1½	38	3.8	18	45.7	39	99.1
1¾	44	4.4	19	48.3	40	101.6
2	51	5.1	20	50.8	41	104.1
2½	64	6.4	21	53.3	42	106.7
3	76	7.6	22	55.9	43	109.2
3½	89	8.9	23	58.4	44	111.8
4	102	10.2	24	61.0	45	114.3
4½	114	11.4	25	63.5	46	116.8
5	127	12.7	26	66.0	47	119.4
6	152	15.2	27	68.6	48	121.9
7	178	17.8	28	71.1	49	124.5
8	203	20.3	29	73.7	50	127.0

yards to meters									
yards	meters	yards	meters	yards	meters	yards	meters	yards	meters
⅛	0.11	2⅛	1.94	4⅛	3.77	6⅛	5.60	8⅛	7.43
⅛	0.11	2⅛	1.94	4⅛	3.77	6⅛	5.60	8⅛	7.43
¼	0.23	2¼	2.06	4¼	3.89	6¼	5.72	8¼	7.54
⅜	0.34	2⅜	2.17	4⅜	4.00	6⅜	5.83	8⅜	7.66
⅝	0.46	2½	2.29	4½	4.11	6½	5.94	8½	7.77
⅝	0.57	2⅝	2.40	4⅝	4.23	6⅝	6.06	8⅝	7.89
¾	0.69	2¾	2.51	4¾	4.34	6¾	6.17	8¾	8.00
⅞	0.80	2⅞	2.63	4⅞	4.46	6⅞	6.29	8⅞	8.12
1	0.91	3	2.74	5	4.57	7	6.40	9	8.23
1¼	1.03	3¼	2.86	5⅛	4.69	7¼	6.52	9⅛	8.34
1¼	1.14	3¼	2.97	5¼	4.80	7¼	6.63	9¼	8.46
1⅜	1.26	3⅜	3.09	5⅜	4.91	7⅜	6.74	9⅜	8.57
1½	1.37	3½	3.20	5½	5.03	7½	6.86	9½	8.69
1⅝	1.49	3⅝	3.31	5⅝	5.14	7⅝	6.97	9⅝	8.80
1¾	1.60	3¾	3.43	5¾	5.26	7¾	7.09	9¾	8.92
1⅞	1.71	3⅞	3.54	5⅞	5.37	7⅞	7.20	9⅞	9.03
2	1.83	4	3.66	6	5.49	8	7.32	10	9.14

Credits

Concept Editor: Jennifer Gibbs
Production Editor: Lisa Anderson
Photographer: Zac Williams
Stylist: Annie Hampton
Graphic Illustrator: Kim Coxey
Book Designer: Heather Harcourt

Index